JEREMIAH

EPWORTH PREACHER'S COMMENTARIES

★

JEREMIAH

★

JOSEPH WOODS
M.A.

LONDON : THE EPWORTH PRESS

FIRST PUBLISHED 1964

© THE EPWORTH PRESS 1964

Book Steward
FRANK H. CUMBERS

SET IN MONOTYPE TIMES ROMAN AND PRINTED IN
GREAT BRITAIN BY THE CAMELOT PRESS LTD
LONDON AND SOUTHAMPTON

To the men of
Trinity United Theological College
Umuahia, Eastern Nigeria

General Introduction

WE are living in a day in which the authority and message of the Bible is being rediscovered and declared. Preachers are realizing afresh that their message must be based on the Word of God in Scripture. Many commentaries on the books of the Bible are already available, and give much space to the consideration of critical questions and historical and literary problems.

This new series of commentaries, as its name suggests, is written specifically for preachers, and particularly for those who feel themselves ill-equipped to study the more advanced works of scholarship. Its aim is to set forth the essential message of the Bible. Questions of authorship, date, background, will be dealt with briefly, and only in so far as they are necessary for informed preaching. The main purpose of each commentary will be (a) to explain the original meaning of each biblical passage, and (b) to indicate its relevance to human need in the present situation. Bearing in mind this dual purpose, each author will have freedom to use what method of treatment he thinks most suitable to the book of the Bible on which he is commenting.

To save space, the biblical text is not printed, but the commentary is based on that of the *Revised Version*.

The author of this commentary—the twelfth in the series—is the Rev. Joseph Woods, who was a missionary in Eastern Nigeria from 1938 to 1959, and the Principal of Trinity United Theological College, Umuahia, from 1956 to 1959.

Attacking the popular misconception of Jeremiah, Mr Woods shows us the real Jeremiah as, often in agony of mind, he fearlessly declares 'the word of the Lord' to his generation. ('Surely he is a sign that God has set up, to direct us to His own strong, faithful Son'.) Wherever possible, the author dates the prophecies and, by placing them in their 'life situation', shows how relevant and disturbing was the challenge of Jeremiah to his contemporaries. Throughout his commentary, he reminds the preacher that the same 'word of the Lord' is strikingly relevant to us in our times.

GREVILLE P. LEWIS

Preface

IT has not been easy to work within the limits of space essential to a series of commentaries of this type and produce a little book about the longest, and one of the most important, of the prophetic books of the Old Testament. Yet I am glad that a former OT editor of the series, the Rev. Dr Stanley Frost, asked me to try. I have been amazed at the helpfulness and patience of the present OT editors, the Revs. Dr Norman H. Snaith and S. Clive Thexton and the General Editor, the Rev. Greville P. Lewis. Thanks to them this little book is much less inadequate than it might have been.

The commentary had its beginning in a series of 'Bible-readings' during a reunion of former students in the days when I was on the staff of a united theological college in Nigeria. We discovered then how relevant this book is. As the work has proceeded, I have grown even more sure of the importance of Jeremiah. The God who spoke to His prophet in the days of Nebuchadrezzar sees to it that he may still speak in our time.

If this commentary is used to persuade some other preachers to look again at what the Lord has to say through Jeremiah, I believe that they will discover that they have no need to indulge in allegory or mental contortions to become aware of his relevance. All that is required of us is faith, and faithfulness to what stands written about the ways of God with this man, and with men.

JOSEPH WOODS

AUDENSHAW
1964

Abbreviations

*RV*m	Revised Version margin
RSV	Revised Standard Version (Nelson)
NEB	New English Bible
MHB	*The Methodist Hymn-book*
NHS	N. H. Snaith, *The Distinctive Ideas of the Old Testament* (Epworth)
PH	*The Preacher's Handbook*, volumes 1, 2, etc. (Epworth)
TWB	*A Theological Wordbook of the Bible* (SCM)

Introduction

IT is high time that literate people got away from the idea that Jeremiah is the patron saint of the miserable and complaining people whom we dislike. The real Jeremiah has so much to say to us that we must not be put off by people who refuse to let him speak for himself. At a time when we are being urged to move on to 'religionless' Christianity, it is not unimportant to have this prophet's witness to God as the living Lord who insists on setting life right from its innermost core to its outermost layer. Even the 'existentialist' can learn from Jeremiah's insistence that God requires from us constant fresh decisions such as must arise from obedient and continuous attention to His holy will.

The times of Jeremiah

Jeremiah may justifiably be regarded as the finest character that God shaped in OT times. He was probably a descendant of Eli and also of Abiathar, the priest who was deposed by Solomon (1 Kings 2²⁶⁻²⁷). Born about 640 BC at Anathoth, on the northern border of the little kingdom of Judah, he grew up in a country that lay uncomfortably between two great powers, Egypt to the south and the rising power of Babylon to the east.

When God called Jeremiah to prophesy, Assyria was a declining power and was soon to be superseded by Babylon as the main power to the east. Already Judah had been for some time an unwilling satellite of Assyria, but Assyria's growing weakness created a situation in which it was possible for Josiah to ban the worship of Assyrian gods in Judah, as part of his 'reformation' in about 621 BC (Cf. 2 Kings 22¹-23⁵. Chapters 21-5 of 2 Kings are important for an understanding of the times of Jeremiah). Josiah was killed at Megiddo by the Pharaoh of Egypt, in the course of the confused struggle for power that followed the fall of Nineveh, capital of Assyria, in 612 BC. Jehoiakim was put on the throne of Judah by the Egyptians. But Egypt was no longer capable of the role of a 'first-class power', as Jeremiah realized, and soon Judah was once again being controlled from the east. After Egypt's disastrous retreat from Carchemish in 605 BC it should have been clear to everyone that Babylon (or 'Chaldea'), not Egypt, was to be Assyria's successor as the dominant power.

Jeremiah consistently prophesied that this supremacy of Babylon was within the purpose of God. But many prominent leaders in Judah would not see it. The prophet came to be looked on as a traitor because he insisted that it was God's will that Judah should submit to the Babylonians. So, shortly before Jehoiakim died, Judah foolishly rebelled against Babylon. In 597 BC Jehoiakim's unfortunate successor, Jehoiachin, was taken prisoner by the Babylonians and they set Zedekiah in his place. After a time of uneasy submission to Babylon, Zedekiah, misled by Egyptian intrigues and by bad advice from his own counsellors, was himself disloyal to his Babylonian master. So in 586 BC final disaster came upon king and people alike. The kingdom of Judah ceased to exist.

The Babylonians now began to control the ruined state by 'indirect rule' with Gedaliah as 'governor'. But soon Gedaliah was assassinated, the remaining leaders of the community fled in panic to Egypt, and Jeremiah was dragged along with them. Where the prophet died or when is not known; it may have been about 580 BC, though some writers infer from 53[21] that it was 560 BC.

Jeremiah the man

The *Concise Oxford Dictionary* defines a 'jeremiah' as a 'doleful prophet or denouncer of the times'. The preacher must take this proverbial misconception into account. It arose and persisted largely because the prophet was wrongly believed to be the author of *Lamentations*, the book that follows *Jeremiah* in our English versions, though not in the Hebrew OT. So Jeremiah is misunderstood by later generations, as if the misunderstanding of his contemporaries were not enough. The remarkable thing about the prophet is not his dolefulness, in spite of the fact that he was all too well acquainted with grief. What really is notable is Jeremiah's courage—the courage that God gave him. It would not be easy to find anyone who could equal the steadfast endurance he showed for year after year in the face of continual threats and persecution. Loyalty to God required him to proclaim to his own people that the Temple and even the state of Judah would have to be destroyed. Jeremiah went on day by day, month by month, year after year delivering this message which he relished no more than anyone else in Judah. He met at first with derision, then with physical and mental suffering—fightings without and fears within—and eventually he found that attacks on his life were being planned and made by powerful people. It is not surprising that Jeremiah was driven from the home and kindred he loved so greatly; it is not surprising that he was persecuted and well-nigh martyred; the miracle is that the Lord brought this loyal son of Judah through all this and sustained in him the faith that, even though Jerusalem itself must fall, 'the city of God remaineth'.

In this prophet, then, we are given one of God's clearest demonstrations, before the time when 'the Word became flesh', that a human life can be made the best means of revealing His purposes. 'Jeremiah's repulse by men drove him to God, and his repulse by God made him draw closer to Him. And thus his life became a fellowship with God, his thoughts and feelings a dialogue between him and God' (A. B. Davidson in Hastings' *Dictionary of the Bible*, II, 578a). The prophet's life came to be governed by the word of God and so, centuries later, some of those who watched Jesus believed that Jeremiah had come back to earth. They were wrong, but they were right to recognize that the life of the great prophet points clearly to Him of whom the high priest was to say 'it is more to your interest that one man should die for the people' (Jn 11 50, *NEB*). Surely, despite his failings and all his struggles and doubts, Jeremiah is a sign for us; in his sufferings and bravery and faith, he is a sign that God has set up, to direct us to His own strong, faithful Son.

The Book of Jeremiah

The material which we know as *Jeremiah* is a rather bewildering collection of sayings and historical and biographical stories. The *RV* is of course translated from the Hebrew, but if we refer to the Greek version of the OT (the *LXX*) we find that much of the material from Chapter 25 onwards is arranged in a different order. A further complication is that the *LXX* has a rather briefer text than the Hebrew. Again, a few fragments incorporated in the book may be derived from other prophets, and there are indications that many of those who collected and arranged the material were men with a strong loyalty to the ideas of *Deuteronomy*, as well as a veneration for Jeremiah. A modern editor, if he were confronted with what we know as *Jeremiah* for the first time, would probably regard these chapters simply as part of the material to be arranged and worked up into a '*Life and Times of Jeremiah the Prophet*'. In a commentary of this nature, it is possible to do little more than to indicate that problems of this type exist. It is an earthen vessel that contains the treasure, and our concern is with the treasure,—what a treasure it is! (See also the note on p. 5 for an attempt to arrange the matter in *Jeremiah* in chronological order.)

A note on books

Preachers will already be aware of the help that is to be gained from one-volume commentaries on the Bible—the Abingdon, the IVF, Gore, Lowther Clarke and the new Peake. There are two 'classic' studies of the book: the *Century Bible* commentary by Peake, and J. Skinner's *Prophecy and Religion* (Cambridge). There is a useful *Torch Commentary* (SCM) by H. Cunliffe-Jones, and H. Wheeler Robinson's treatment of *Jeremiah* in *The Cross in the Old Testament* (also SCM) should not be forgotten. George Adam Smith's *Jeremiah* (Hodder & Stoughton) is particularly interesting for its translation.

There is a helpful chapter by Dr N. H. Snaith on some sections of *Jeremiah* in *PH*(3), pp. 163-90, and H. T. Kuist has written a useful brief commentary in the *Layman's Bible Commentary* series (SCM).

A. C. Welch's *Jeremiah* (Oxford) and the material on *Jeremiah* in *The Interpreter's Bible* are full of insight and have real value, though many will feel that they have to be used with caution because of their very individual approach to some issues.

The *RSV* translation of *Jeremiah* is a useful commentary on the *RV*—by implication, and this will apply also to the *New English Bible* version of *Jeremiah* when the OT is published.

An attempt at a chronological arrangement of the book of Jeremiah

(*A*) When the emperor Asshur-banipal died in 626 BC the power of Assyria was already waning. In 616 BC Nineveh, the capital of Assyria, was besieged by the Chaldeans and the Medes. It was about this time that Jeremiah became aware that new things were stirring. Nineveh fell in 612. An Egyptian army moved north and in 608 Josiah, king of Judah, was killed by the Pharaoh at Megiddo.

Chapters **1-6,** and possibly **11$^{1-17}$** refer to this period.

(*B*) The Egyptians set Jehoiakim on the throne of Judah, but with the retreat of the Egyptians before Nebuchadrezzar in 605 BC it became clear that Babylonia was the dominant power. It was now only a matter of time before Judah came under her control, and she was invaded in 602 BC (cf. 2 Kings 24^2). Three months after the death of Jehoiakim in 598 Jerusalem fell, and Nebuchadrezzar put Zedekiah on the throne.

22$^{10-12}$ and chapters **26** and **47** may be placed early in the reign of Jehoiakim (say 609-605 BC). The period just after the repulse of the Egyptians from Carchemish (say 605-602) is represented by **7^1-8^{22}, 9$^{1-9}$, 19^1-20^{18}, 25$^{1-38}$, 46$^{1-12}$, 36$^{1-32}$, 16$^{1-21}$,** and **45$^{1-5}$.**

9$^{10-22}$, 12$^{7-17}$, 35$^{1-19}$, 21$^{11-12}$ and **49$^{1-6}$** may be linked with the time of the invasion of Judah in 602, and **20$^{1-6}$, 22$^{13-23}$, 5$^{10-21}$, 18$^{1-23}$, 10$^{1-25}$, 11^{18}-12^6,** and **23$^{1-40}$** with the days before the death of Jehoiakim (602-597 BC).

(*C*) From the earlier part of the reign of Zedekiah (about 597-590) we have **15$^{5-9}$, 13$^{15-27}$, 22$^{1-9}$, 24^{-30}, 14^1-15^4, 24$^{1-10}$, 34$^{34-9}$, 27^1-29^{32}, 48$^{1-47}$, 13$^{12-14}$, 17$^{1-27}$** and **21$^{1-10}$.**

The latter part of the reign of Zedekiah (590-586 BC) is reflected in **34$^{1-7}$, 37$^{1-10}$, 34$^{8-22}$, 37$^{11-21}$, 30^1-33^{26}, 38$^{1-28}$.**

(*D*) Lastly, for the governorship of Gedaliah and the period after his assassination, we have **39^1-44^{30}, 49$^{7-33}$, 46$^{13-26}$, 50^1-51^{64}.**

Unless a passage is specifically dated, and not always even then, we have nothing to go on except reasonable conjecture.

Therefore, such an arrangement as is set out here is merely one of several possibilities. But it is important to make some such attempt, if only to insist that prophecy is related to history, and has meaning for the present only because it was directly related to specific events in the past.

Commentary

I. Poems and Sayings of Jeremiah (1¹-25³⁸).

1¹⁻³: The 'Title Page'

This section corresponds to the title page of a modern book, but this title does not fit the present form of the book. The editors date the prophecies of Jeremiah as from about 626 to 586 BC, but the book as we now have it certainly contains material from times after 586 BC; e.g. **42¹-44³⁰**. The title may have been reasonably appropriate for some early collection of material which formed the nucleus of the book as we now have it, and the discrepancy may be due to the fact that no adjustment was made to this title by later editors.

Some recent writers doubt the accuracy of the date given for the beginning of Jeremiah's prophesying, '*the thirteenth year*' of Josiah's reign which is 626 BC. At the time of Josiah's 'Reformation' in 621 BC, Jeremiah does not seem to be at all a prominent figure in Judah, and this requires explanation if he had already been prophesying in Jerusalem for four or five years. It may well be argued that Jeremiah started to prophesy some time after 621 and before 612 BC. Nineveh, capital of Assyria, fell to the Medes and Chaldeans in 612. The reverberations of that crash were soon felt all over the former Assyrian Empire, and from 612 onwards Jeremiah could hardly have been in doubt about the identity of the 'foe from the north' which the Lord would use to chastise His people. (On the other side, there is still strong support for the date 626 among scholars who believe that passages like **8⁸⁻¹³** and chapter **11** are closely connected with the events of 621 BC.)

1¹. '*Hilkiah*'. This is not the Hilkiah of 2 Kings 22⁸ who would be a Zadokite, whereas '*the priests that were in Anathoth*' were descendants of Abiathar.

'*Anathoth*'. This village was very near to the capital, about three miles north-east of Jerusalem; cf. 2 Kings 2²⁶⁻⁷.

Jeremiah's home was '*in the land of Benjamin*', on the northern border of the little kingdom of Judah, and it was natural for him to develop an interest in the future of what had once been the neighbouring kingdom of Israel.

1³. '*Jehoiakim*'. Josiah was in fact succeeded by Jehoahaz who reigned for a mere three months before the Egyptians set Jehoiakim in his place; cf. **22¹⁰⁻¹²**.

'*Zedekiah*'. Jehoiakim (608-597 BC) was succeeded by Jehoiachin who also ruled only for three months, before he was deposed and exiled. This time it was the Babylonians who intervened and they put Zedekiah on the throne (cf. **13¹⁸⁻¹⁹**). He was to be the last of the kings of Judah, ruling from 597 to the fall of his capital and '*the carrying away of Jerusalem captive*' in 586 BC.

The '*words of Jeremiah*' (**1¹**) are important only because the prophet is someone to whom '*the word of the Lord*' (**1²**) came at a particular stage in the story of God's people. Some people understandably become deeply interested in Jeremiah's mental processes and emotions, but the Bible is not greatly concerned with such matters. The central concern is '*the word of the Lord*' which '*came*' to the prophet, which kept coming to him: '*the words of Jeremiah*' have significance only because they are an attempt to declare the word of the Lord which came to him in those critical times.

The name 'Jeremiah' probably means 'God hurls' (though some scholars prefer to translate 'God exalts'), and it is very appropriate for a prophet who was often flung into situations which he would gladly have avoided. This home-loving, sociable man was 'hurled' into situations where he was certain to incur the contempt and hatred of other people, even of his own neighbours and kinsmen; this great lover of his country was thrown into the position of having to advise her to surrender to a hated invader. Yet, because it was God who hurled him, Jeremiah was given all the strength that he needed to face hatred and loneliness, isolation and danger. We have not to look far in the history of the Church for examples of men 'hurled' by God into difficult places. It can happen still, and God can be trusted still to supply what is needed. It is when preachers start hurling themselves into situations that trouble comes!

The responsibility given to the prophet is given also to every preacher—first to let the word of the Lord 'come' to him, and then to proclaim it in ways that men can understand, in his own words. The hope and the fear given to the prophet are given also to a preacher, the hope and the fear that through his words '*the word of the Lord*' will be made known to other men—the word of the Love that judges perfectly and that saves to the uttermost.

1⁴⁻¹⁰: A man thrust forth by God

Even before his birth Jeremiah has been set apart by the Lord to be His prophet to the nations. He protests that he is not senior enough for such heavy responsibility, but God insists that, immature as he is, he will have all the necessary authority because He has determined to make His will known through His prophet.

1⁵. '*sanctified*'. This is the only use of this term in connection with a prophet in the OT (cf. Jn 10³⁶).

As in *Amos*, the call of the prophet is described simply as a conversation between himself and God (notice '*me*' in verse 4). It was only because '*the word of the Lord came*' that a man was enlightened and also empowered to be a prophet. God chose him and moulded his nature and his life from the beginning for this task (verse 5). Although men may regard him as a mere junior, subordinate and insignificant, God is determined to use him; cf. Job 32⁴⁻¹⁰. Out of the mouths of those whom the world regards as 'babes and sucklings' the Lord can ordain strength (cf. Ezek 3⁴, ⁹, Lk 12⁴⁻⁵). Because God has '*touched*' the mouth of Jeremiah and put his '*words*' into it (verse 9), the work which the prophet has to do is the concern of all '*nations*' and '*kingdoms*' (verse 10; cf. **28⁸**). God's word will not return to Him void but will do His work in the breaking down and building up of nations (verse 10). Jeremiah is not appointed to concoct and say something clever and interesting; his calling is simply to the task of interpreting what will be achieved by the Lord. The prophet is to be an overseer, a man '*set . . . over the nations and over the kingdoms*'.

Jeremiah is a true prophet who was nearly lost in a time of false prophets. He would have preferred 'security' and the pleasures of living at peace with his kinsfolk and his village neighbours, but God convinces him that the life he has to lead and the work he has to do are not his own but God's. Then he is hurled into a career of strife and suffering and danger. But when God calls men He also equips them for their calling; because Jeremiah has been chosen by God, his arduous career is also one of remarkable courage and strange beauty (cf. verse 8; 2 Cor 12[9]; Heb 11[32-4]).

A prophet is 'a man who speaks to men on behalf of God' and therefore Jeremiah was equipped by both heredity and environment to deliver the Lord's message with his lips and with his life. By his speech and his manner of life he made it plain that the will of God was closely concerned, not only with the morals, but also with the politics and economics of the kingdom of Judah. When the word of the Lord comes to God's people in our own generation it is still addressed, through the power of the Holy Spirit, to the '*nations*', to our own nation as well as others. The words of Jeremiah still witness to the fact that God's way is the only way to justice and peace, and that every manifestation of human selfishness stands under His judgement. The word which came to Jeremiah still condemns those attitudes and activities and failures in cooperation among the nations which lie at the root of so much poverty and hunger and disease.

The man who has never been tempted to run away from God has never met the true God. But those who give way to the temptation to run away will have no true peace or joy until they do what God calls them to do. We sometimes try to set feeble excuses against the plain call of God (cf. verse 6); we imagine that we are being modest, or we plead a lack of qualification or strength or ability, when we may in fact be doubting and mistrusting the power of God to provide for His own work.

Preachers will realize that many people need to be helped to understand *how* the call of God comes today, and how it may be recognized; cf. W. E. Sangster, *The Approach to Preaching*, Chapter 1. But when the call comes, it is a source of great confidence to know that the Lord of all life has moulded our lives from the very beginning, and when the task is hard and distasteful it is a source of great comfort to know that He never pulls down except to build better (Cf. Jn 3[16-21]).

While in affliction's furnace,
And passing through the fire,
Thy love we praise,
Which knows our days
And ever brings us nigher . . .
The love divine
Which made us Thine
Shall keep us Thine for ever.   (*MHB* 411)

1¹¹⁻¹⁹: Two signs

God uses a rod of 'wake-tree' wood to show Jeremiah that He is wakeful, however much may point to the contrary. Then He uses a pot boiling over a fire fanned by the north wind to show His prophet that danger is threatening Judah from that quarter. The enemy must rule in Jerusalem, the holy city, and so God will discipline His idolatrous people. Such a message is sure to set all sections of the people against Jeremiah, but God will fortify him against every kind of opposition.

1¹¹ ¹². Everything here depends on the play on two Hebrew words, cf. RVm. An almond-tree in Hebrew is 'shaked' (the waker) and God uses a rod of this tree to show the prophet that He Himself is 'shoked' (wakeful). The tree is called 'shaked' because it does wake early, in January or February. A modern prophet in a tropical country who was not afraid of puns might say 'I saw a *mango* tree, and the word came to me, "How can a *man go* unless he is sent?".'

1¹³. '*a seething caldron . . . from the north.*' RSV is helpful here: 'a boiling pot, facing away from the north'—so that it would boil over on the south.

1¹⁵. Only a victorious conqueror could set his '*throne*' in front of the '*gates of Jerusalem*', and he would do this in order to judge the defeated people.

1¹⁶. '*And I will utter . . .*'. God also is going to judge them.
   '*burned incense*'. Here and elsewhere (in *Jer*) this phrase means 'to offer sacrifice', and the reference is probably to

the smoke of burnt offerings. In 6²⁰, 17²⁶, 41⁵ and possibly 44²¹, however, the reference is to frankincense.

1¹⁷. '*gird up thy loins*'. He must tuck up the skirts of his robes in order to be ready for work. A modern idiomatic equivalent would be 'Get your jacket off and roll up your sleeves'. (I have often seen Moslems in W. Africa 'gird up their loins' in order to ride a bicycle!)

1¹⁸. '*brasen walls*'. More accurately 'walls of bronze'.

We are given no date for this section in the text and conjecture only is possible. If the prophet's call came in the latter years of the reign of Josiah (see commentary on 1¹⁻³), these signs may belong to the opening of the reign of Jehoiakim, when it was clear that Jeremiah must soon meet opposition from the palace and religious officials and from ordinary people in Jerusalem and the towns of Judah (cf. verses 18-19).

To the prophet, the significance of the '*rod*' of 'wake-wood' or almond is that, even if the faithless conduct of the people of Judah seems to be allowed to go on unchecked, in fact everything is watched and controlled by the Lord. He neither slumbers nor sleeps and His word is powerfully effective. God is always wide awake, to judge,—and to save (cf. 31²⁸, 44²⁷, Ps 121). Jeremiah would be aware of the tradition concerning Aaron's almond rod, which is the sign of God's wrath against the rebellious (cf. Num 17⁸, Ezek 7¹⁰⁻¹¹).

The pot tilted towards the south in verse 13 is pictured as boiling over a field-oven which is closed in on three sides and open only to the north, the quarter from which the wind is blowing. It has been the fashion among commentators to give a lot of space to a discussion of the identity of these enemies in the '*north*': were they Scythians or Chaldeans or some other people? Some scholars now consider that the evidence for a Scythian threat to Judah is so flimsy that we can leave them out of the discussion for the future. If Jeremiah was able at all to put a name to the enemy at this stage, it was probably the Chaldeans that he had in mind. So much depends on the date of the sign, and at that we can only guess, and it may well be that at this point in his career the prophet could do no more than indicate that God's instrument for disciplining Judah would come from the '*north*', and not from Egypt in the south.

The far north was regarded as a mysterious place from which there came supernatural terrors, and the vague phrase '*all the families of the kingdoms of the north*' (verse 15) may have been designed in the first instance to strike fear into those who had to be warned, in the hope that they might change their attitude to the Lord (cf. 4⁶, 6¹, 10²², 50⁴¹⁻², Isa 14¹³, Joel 2²⁰).

Obedience to the Lord is not going to mean that the prophet will be popular, or even that he will be respected; he is promised deliverance, not from persecution and suffering, but from being defeated by persecution and suffering (verse 19). Only the fear of the Lord will save him from fear of his congregations (verse 17). He will have to learn that 'one man with God is a majority'. In trust and in courage will be his strength. He is going to find that the best of all is that God is '*with*' him (verse 19; cf. Josh 1⁹).

The preacher will notice that this chapter is a demonstration of the way in which God comes to men. His word comes in specific situations and has then to be put into human terms, into words, but also into deeds. It is interesting to notice that the first words of the book may be translated 'The *acts* of Jeremiah'. Through heredity and environment, God shapes earthen vessels into which He will put His treasure, and those vessels are important for what they do and for what they are, as well as for what they say. Jeremiah's sermons and poetic utterances are important, but his whole attitude towards people who are in rebellion against their Lord is also a word from God to them. God gives the prophet a message to deliver, and He also gives him the courage to deliver it, and the strength to withstand the reaction it provokes. So, from the outset, there is a sense in which the Lord's prophet is being taught by Him that the Word has not only to be put into words, but has also to *become flesh*.

God is always awake and active on our behalf, and He gives His prophets to us to remind us that we have a Lord and Saviour who makes Himself known in His activity. However much we may be tempted to suspect that God is not awake, His witnesses insist that this world was made by Him and He continues to work in it (cf. Jn 5¹⁷). It is because this world is His in every part that God may choose to speak through little things like dry sticks and boiling pans, as well as through the rise and fall of kingdoms and empires. It is no business of the prophet to be a sort of ventriloquist and make these things speak something that sounds like a word from God; his responsibility is to bear witness to the fact that God Himself has chosen to speak, now through this means and now through that.

We are not Hebrew prophets, but the things that happen around us also are stamped with the mark of a living, watchful Lord in whose hands lies the sure, ultimate destruction of evil. Followers of Jesus Christ may, and should, keep open their eyes for the signs of the times; to ignore them, while the nations to which we belong are trying to commit suicide, is not holiness but blindness of heart. God still is pleased to make Himself known in the rough and tumble of everyday life (cf. Jn 17¹⁵). But this knowledge that approaches us is very different from the kind of knowledge that we can 'master' with our own brains; this Truth that speaks to us requires our obedient service, and the witness of our whole heart and soul and strength (cf. Jn 17¹⁷). Every witness to this Truth is always a learner; he has to 'follow on to know the Lord' (Hos 6³). He is being taught all the time, discovering from the way the Lord deals with him something of His character, and therefore something of the character that He requires in, and confers on, His spokesmen. The obedient witness learns that to serve this Lord is to serve all the nations. And he learns to rejoice with Luther that 'where and with whom God speaks, be it in anger or in grace, that man is assuredly immortal. The Person of God who thus speaks, and the Word of God, indicate that we are such creatures as God would speak with in eternity and in an immortal way.'

(In these paragraphs I am to some extent dependent on my study, *The OT in the Church* (SPCK, 1949). See especially pp. 20-33.)

2¹⁻³: Look on this picture . . .

The Lord sends Jeremiah to remind Jerusalem of the 'honeymoon' days in the desert when He kept His faithful people secure.

2². '*kindness*'. The Hebrew word is *chesed* which here stands for the loyal devotion which is a reflection of, and a response to, the completely trustworthy love of God. Cf. 3^{12}, where the word describes the character of the Lord Himself and is translated '*merciful*', and 9^{23-4}, where it is translated '*loving kindness*'.

2^3. '*all that devour him . . .*'. Read, 'all those who devoured her were held guilty; evil came upon them, says the Lord'. Israel was so clearly the Lord's special possession that anyone who interfered with her was guilty of sacrilege and had to take the consequences.

In 2^1-6^{30} we have a collection of some of Jeremiah's finest poems. Perhaps these were assembled in written form in about 603 BC as a record of the type of prophecy which he was delivering in the period before King Josiah was killed (cf. 36^{27-32}). In these chapters there are several indications that Jeremiah has been influenced by the teaching of Hosea and the picture of the wilderness period in verses 2-3 agrees with *Hosea* instead of with the traditions accepted elsewhere. (Contrast Hos 2^{2-20} with Num 14^1 and Ezek 20^{5-9}, 23^{1-3}.)

This passage, from the words '*I remember . . .*', is in verse. It is helpful to consult a translation such as the *RSV* where the layout of the printing makes a distinction between prose and verse sections.

This is an oracle 'concerning' (notice *RV*m of verse 2) the loyal devotion of the people to their Lord in the days when they were '*in the wilderness*' after their deliverance from bondage in Egypt. When God gave His covenant to Israel, she became His Bride. (This is the metaphor implied in '*the love of thine espousals*' and in the parallel and synonymous expression '*the kindness of thy youth*'.) At first she responded to God's utterly reliable *chesed* with a steadfast faithfulness. She knew Him as the Saviour, the Bridegroom who had saved His bride into a situation where she delighted to do His will, where her own strong devotion was a clear reflection of His completely trustworthy love. In the '*land that was not sown*' there were no agricultural gods, no baals, none of the fertility gods of Canaan to tempt her into unfaithfulness. Like every good wife she '*went after*' her husband; she was happy to have the Lord, her Bridegroom, in front of her to deal with the dangers of the way (cf. 2^{32}, $3^{1, 14}$, 31^{32}).

In verse 3 there is another metaphor: God's people are the

'*firstfruits*' of His harvest. They are '*holiness unto the Lord*',
His special property and taboo to man, so that He sent evil
on anyone who tried to injure them. It was not impossible
for them to get into trouble, but they were never in danger
of destruction, since nothing could separate them from the
chesed of God. In those honeymoon days, Israel knew that
she was 'holy', a people set apart by God to know the benefits
of His saving love, a people preserved from destruction in order
that she might do her Lord's will (cf. Deut 26[1-11], Hos 9[10],
Ezek 48[14]).

It is not only Jeremiah who is called; now the prophet
is shown what is the high calling of his fellowmen who are
God's people. They are '*firstfruits*', the beginning of the harvest
that He will gather from all the earth (cf. Ezek 16[1-14]); they
are His Bride, a community whose nature depends entirely
on its relationship with the Bridegroom who is its Saviour.
These metaphors still have significance for God's people,
the Church:

> *From heaven He came and sought her*
> *To be His holy bride;*
> *With His own blood He bought her,*
> *And for her life He died.* (*MHB* 701)

Just as God bound His covenant-Bride to Himself by the
Exodus which He brought about in the days of Moses, so He
has bound the Church to Himself as the Bride of the New
Covenant by another Exodus, accomplished at Jerusalem
in the days of Pontius Pilate (notice that the word translated
'decease' or 'departure' (*RV*m) in Lk 9[31] is in fact the Greek
word 'exodus'). The Church also is 'holy', belonging to God
as a 'kind of firstfruits of his creatures' (Jas 1[18]). It is the community of those who are called to be the means of carrying
His 'salvation unto the end of the earth', until all is safely
gathered in (cf. Isa 49[6]).

2[4-28]: . . . and on this

God's people have forgotten His saving love. They have
changed their allegiance, so that their 'worship' of Him is
really a cloak for idolatry. This ungrateful change of loyalty
means that they are courting disaster. Already there have

been troubles enough to provide an unmistakable warning; yet they still show no sign of real repentance.

2⁴. '*Jacob . . . Israel*' (cf. verses 14, 16, 28). One cannot always be certain in this section whether such names stand for the former kingdom of Israel, or for the people of the kingdom of Judah, or for both. Although Jeremiah is chiefly concerned with the people of Judah, he had grown up in the '*land of Benjamin*' (1¹) and was interested in the northern tribes who had been conquered by Assyria a century earlier. There are good reasons for believing that much of the territory of the northern kingdom was brought under the control of the kingdom of Judah in the latter part of the reign of Josiah.

2⁶. '*shadow of death*'. Follow *RV*m and translate 'deep dark- ness' (cf. Ps 23⁴).

2⁸. '*rulers*' is correct here, not 'pastors' as in *AV* (see *RV*m). In *Jeremiah*, the 'shepherd' is always a ruler (cf. 3¹⁵, 10²¹, 12¹⁰, 22²², 23¹⁻²). It is worth notice that the 'Good Shepherd', who is the 'Shepherd of Israel, and mine', is certainly not a farm employee, but is a Ruler, the Lord and Owner of His flock.

2⁹. '*plead*'. Better 'contend' (*RSV*). The point is that the Lord will assert His rights against them.

2¹⁰. '*isles of Kittim*' means the 'shores of Cyprus', while '*Kedar*' refers to an Arab tribe of the desert to the east of Judah (cf. 49²⁸⁻⁹). Whether one looks east or west, to the farthest horizon, there can be seen no parallel to Israel's amazing change of loyalty.

2¹³. '*two evils*'. Not only have they deserted the Lord who is '*their glory*' (verse 11), but they have also presumed to think that they can construct their own substitutes for Him.

'*living waters*'. This refers to water that is continually flow- ing, bubbling from a good spring or gushing out of a rock. Rainwater collected from the roofs was stored underground in '*cisterns*' cut out of the rock, and if they were '*broken*' these provided a dwindling, brackish supply, which was liable to fail when it was most needed. The metaphor is a vivid way of telling people to whom water is so precious that they are committing suicide by leaving the living God and making their own useless idols.

2¹⁴. '*homeborn*'. The child of slave parents was different from the '*servant*' who had been enslaved later in life. Israel is neither of these; he was delivered from slavery in Egypt to be '*holiness unto the Lord*' (verse 3), so why is he now subjected to foreigners—'*why is he become a prey*'? The answer is given in verses 17-19.

2¹⁵. '*young lions*'. A metaphor for Egypt or, more probably, Assyria.

2¹⁶. '*Noph*'. This is the Egyptian city of Memphis and with '*Tahpanhes*' (cf. **43⁷⁻¹⁰**) it indicates domination by Egypt. This section may be connected with the time after the death of Josiah and the deposition of Jehoahaz, when Judah, having become free of Assyria, was forced to submit to Egyptian control (cf. 2 Kings 23²⁹⁻³⁵).

2¹⁸. '*Shihor*', '*the River*'. Follow *RV*m.

2²⁰. '*I have broken*'. Read with *RV*m, '*thou hast broken*' (cf. Mt 11²⁹⁻³⁰).
'*high hill . . . green tree*'. These were the sites favoured for Canaanite cults (cf. **3¹⁶, 17²**).

2²¹. Israel was the '*noble vine*' of the Lord, but the graft has died and now the old crude stock, '*the degenerate plant*', is flourishing (cf. **23⁵**, Isa 5¹⁻⁷, Ps 80⁸⁻⁹, Jn 15¹⁻⁶).

2²². '*lye*'. An alkaline substance obtained from ashes, similar to kitchen soda.
'*marked*'. Better, 'ingrained'.

2²³. '*Baalim*'. The plural of baal.
'*the valley*'. See **7³¹** and 2 Kings 23¹⁰.
'*dromedary*'. Follow *RV*m, 'a young camel'.

2²⁴. '*in her occasion*'. During the mating season, which is '*her month*'.

2²⁵. '*Withold thy foot . . . thirst*'. 'Do not wear your sandals out and work up a raging thirst' by chasing in a passion after false gods.

2²⁷. '*stock*'. A tree or wooden pole was often associated with the goddess Asherah, but here the word seems to represent an object connected with some male deity who can be addressed as '*father*'. The '*stone*' (the same word is translated in some other places as 'image') was a pillar, the mazzebah (cf. 3⁹, Deut 16²¹⁻²).

2²⁸. '*according to the number . . .*'. There are as many gods in Judah as there are cities!

Jeremiah was well acquainted with what was going on at the local shrines, and in the Temple. The rites that were being practised were a mixed form of worship, an attempt to keep in with the gods of Canaan and of Judah's powerful neighbours, as well as with the Lord. Worship of the gods of the land involved licentious practices, fertility rites and 'sacred' prostitution, which revealed a complete misunderstanding of the character of the Lord and a virtual disregard of the covenant relationship into which He has entered with His people. These things arise because of forgetfulness of what He has done, because of ingratitude (verses 5-7). God's people have turned away from life to emptiness and now it is a case of the blind leading the blind (verse 8). The Lord alone is the fountain of life, and those who turn away from Him are choosing to die in a bondage like that from which He delivered their fathers. They are exchanging the liberty He gave them to do His will for slavery to their own feelings and desires. It is because they have no proper fear of God (verses 19-20) that they rebel, and the end of their sin is '*evil*' and '*bitter*', its wages is death. Sin is always a refusal to acknowledge that God's people exist only to do His will, and such disloyalty as they are showing can only lead to a prostitution of all their gifts (verse 20) till they reach a point where their iniquity is so ingrained that even the most efficient detergent will not touch it (verse 22, cf. 13²³). They have thrown away even the capacity to respond to any appeal from the true God (verse 25): they have abandoned the capacity to hope when they abandon their covenant-faith and love towards Him.

Whether or not these poems reflect conditions in Judah in the months following the death of Josiah (cf. note on verse 16), they would apply, as Jeremiah knew full well, to almost any period since the settlement of the tribes in Canaan. The Israelite who would have no truck with any god but the Lord was always very rare. The general view was that it was only bigots who could take up such a position, now that it was necessary to work out one's beliefs in an environment very different from the wilderness. In Canaan it was commonsense to do as the Canaanites did, and to recognize that the world is influenced by many good and evil powers who all deserve to be acknowledged and feared. 'The natural fertility of Syria . . . intoxicated her immigrants with nature worship . . . while to make confusion worse confounded, the influence of the powerful idolatries were met and combined upon her' (George Adam Smith, *Historical Geography of the Holy Land*, 1906). As the prophets saw it, the trouble was not that God's people were irreligious, but that they were over-religious. They were so busy being 'religious' that they failed to see the great gulf between their religion and the righteousness of the Lord. What they regarded as a proper keeping up with the times, as progress and the advance of civilisation, was in fact a headlong rush in the wrong direction, back to the fleshpots of Egypt.

This chapter points us to a deeper understanding of the nature and the consequences of our sin. Often we reject God's way and trust our own standards; that means that we begin to spend our energies on trying to push a car that could carry us. People are busy today, as they were in Jeremiah's time, looking for an escape in a turbulent world. Today also there are false gods: success, security, popularity, sex, nature, and many others have their following. It is not unknown for people now to turn to amulets and astrology, to spiritism and theosophy, to psychological techniques, to methods of meditation and worship which are expected to make life seem less demanding and uncomfortable. Some make a god of the 'life force' or of the sum of human ideals; others use what they think is 'Christianity' as if it were opium; and all these devices can be ways of turning one's back on the only God, the completely trustworthy Lord and Saviour in whom is our peace (cf. 2 Tim 2¹³). These devices are deceivers whose futility may not be exposed until trouble comes (cf. verse

28); they are always ultimately unsatisfying, empty and worthless. Men soon become like the gods that they worship (verse 5) and we must be thankful that God's wrath always works to turn us back to Himself (verse 19). If we submit to His judgement until we burn with shame for our disloyalty and repent, we shall find that it is no longer true that '*there is no hope*' (verse 25), but that God has provided the answer to our ingrained sin in a new creation (cf. 2 Cor 5¹⁷).

> *Purge me from every evil blot;*
> *My idols all be cast aside;*
> *Cleanse me from every sinful thought,*
> *From all the filth of self and pride.* (*MHB* 562)

2²⁹-3⁵: The wages of disloyalty

Egypt will be no more help to Judah than Assyria was. God's people have not benefited from His discipline. In spite of the drought which He sent to warn them, they are still worshipping in disgusting, heathen ways. In fact they are shameless; they think that they have no need of repentance.

2²⁹. '*plead with*'. This is better translated 'complain against' (cf. *RSV*). They are criticizing and grumbling about God's attitude to them.

2³⁰. '*devoured your prophets*'. They have destroyed the true prophets, but not those who serve the baal (verse 8). Cf. 26²⁰⁻³.

2³¹. The Lord who once led them through the wilderness and a land of deep darkness (verse 6) is now Himself accused of being '*a wilderness*' and '*a land of thick darkness*' by those who have '*broken loose*' to go their own way.

2³². '*attire*'. This refers to the sash which a woman wore to indicate that she was married (cf. Isa 49¹⁸).

2³⁴. Here, as *RV*m shows, the Hebrew is obscure. The point may be that, while bloodshed may sometimes be unavoidable (cf. Ex 22²), there is no justification for their bloodshedding, which is downright evil.

c

2³⁶. '*ashamed of Egypt*'. This may refer to the early part of the reign of Jehoiakim who was put on the throne by the Egyptians.

2³⁷. '*hands upon thine head*'. The gesture indicates complete despair (cf. 2 Sam 13¹⁹), and here probably indicates that she will become a prisoner of war.

3¹. As *RV*m suggests, some words may have been lost from the Hebrew text at the beginning of this verse.

'*yet return*'. This should be translated as a question: 'yet dost thou think that thou mayest come back to me?' (cf. *RV*m). A husband would not take back his unfaithful wife unless he had convincing evidence that she had changed her ways, but God's unfaithful people expect Him to take them back although they are by no means repentant (cf. Deut 24¹⁻⁴).

3². '*bare heights*', '*lien with*'. The barren hilltops were often the place chosen for fertility rites; she cannot point to a single one of them where she has not been 'lain with'.

'*as an Arabian*'. Like a Bedouin bandit on the lookout for defenceless travellers.

3³. '*latter rain*'. The heavy downpours at the end of the rainy season in March and April.

3⁴. '*My father*'. A young wife might so address her husband.

Broken loyalties are not so easily dealt with as God's unfaithful people would like to believe. If only, instead of destroying His messengers, this generation would hear and heed the word of the Lord (2³¹)! Their land which was once flowing with milk and honey is now subject to drought, but they are past shame (3³). They imagine that they have only to coax God by speaking to Him as if they were still His affectionate young bride and then all will be well once more: 'He will forgive— that's His job'.

But Jeremiah knows that a right relationship with the Lord can come only when they abandon everything that is incompatible with the absolute trust and wholehearted obedience that they owe to Him. God would not be God if He treated evil lightly; His righteous love requires reconciliation and atonement. A flippant attitude to His forgiveness (3³⁻⁵) can only lead to hardness of heart (2³⁵; cf. Jn 9⁴¹). What is needed is the will to be loyal and to serve Him 'with a single heart and eye' (*MHB* 572). God has grudged us nothing: He will not be satisfied until we give Him everything (cf. Ps 44¹⁻⁸). Forgetfulness or contempt for what God has done and is doing (2³⁰⁻²) and trust in human powers (2³⁶) can only lead to gross injustice and to ultimate disaster (2³⁴, ³⁷, 3³).

Everything hinges on whether we *know* the Lord (cf. 2⁸). If we do, it follows that:

(*a*) We recognize that our disloyalty to Him and our refusal to obey Him is the central problem for mankind, the problem of sin.

(*b*) We recognize that the only cure for sin is a radical revolution which we cannot bring about ourselves.

(*c*) We find that God can do what is necessary. He is in control of the universe and of history and He is able to make us new.

3⁶-4²: Hope for Israel

When the northern kingdom of Israel refused to repent, she was punished. Judah saw this; yet she also refuses to repent, in anything but name. Her 'reform' is a sham and a fraud. Therefore the people of the northern kingdom will be given another chance and they are promised that Jerusalem shall again be the throne of the Lord, a city where Judah and Israel together shall walk in His way, and then all the nations shall be gathered in.

3⁶. '*high mountain*', '*green tree*', '*harlot*'. See commentary on 2²⁰ and 3².

'*Israel*' here means the old northern kingdom which, before its destruction, had been guilty of the licentious worship of false gods, even as Judah is now.

'*in the days of Josiah*'. It was probably at the time when Josiah was able to extend his authority northwards, beyond the normal boundaries of Judah, that the prophet began to have hopes of the restoration of the northern part of the kingdom.

3⁹. '*through the lightness of her whoredom*'. Probably means 'because she took such an easy view of her unfaithfulness'.

'*stones*' and '*stocks*'. Pillars and poles were regarded as the trysting place of the gods and the goddesses (see commentary on 2²⁷ and cf. Hos 4¹⁷).

3¹⁰. '*feignedly*'. This is important if it represents the prophet's assessment of the attitude of the people of Judah to the reforms which Josiah made in religious practices (cf. verse 6). Judah pretended to *turn back*, but in fact her *back* is still *turned* to the Lord.

3¹². '*the north*'. The message of hope is to be addressed to the people of the former kingdom of Israel who have now been in subjection for a century.

'*I am merciful*'. The reference is to the Lord's *chesed*, His faithfulness to His covenant.

3¹³. '*the strangers*'. This refers to alien *gods*, the Canaanite deities of the land.

3¹⁴. '*I am a husband to you*'. Or 'I am married to you' (*AV*).

'*family*'. Here this stands for a 'clan', a group which might well be as big as a '*city*'.

3¹⁵. '*shepherds*'. See commentary on 2⁸.

3¹⁶. They will not 'miss' (*RV*m) the '*ark*', above which the Lord was believed to be enthroned, since '*the throne of the Lord*' will now be Jerusalem itself (verse 17. Cf. Isa 66¹; Ezek 43⁷). Therefore the ark shall not be 'made any more' (follow *RV*m).

If the ark was still in the Temple, as some think this passage implies, it would be in the care of Zadokite priests, men for whom Jeremiah's relatives (descendants of Abiathar) would have little regard. But the ark does not seem to have been mentioned in the document which influenced Josiah's reforms, and it may have disappeared at a time much earlier than the age of Jeremiah.

3¹⁷. '*stubbornness*'. This word is very characteristic of Jeremiah. It stands for that callousness and blindness of heart which is the consequence of habitually disregarding God and taking one's own way instead (cf. 7²⁴, 9¹⁴, 11⁸, 13¹⁰, 16¹², 18¹², 23¹⁷).

3¹⁸. '*together*'. The implication is that it is only after Judah also has been exiled that Israel will be restored (cf. 50⁴⁻⁵, Ezek 37¹⁵⁻²⁸, Isa 11¹²).

3¹⁹. '*How shall I put thee among the children*'. Read, 'How I long to put thee among my sons' (see *RV*m and cf. Job 42¹⁵).

3²¹. '*the bare heights*'. Instead of a 'noisy throng' (*RV*m of verse 23) busy with licentious rites, the hilltops now echo to sounds of remorse coming from those who believe themselves to be without any hope (cf. 7²⁹).

3²⁴. '*shameful thing*'. This refers to the baal, and the '*flocks . . . herds . . . sons and . . . daughters*' are the animal and human sacrifices which have been offered to false gods (cf. 11¹³, Hos 2¹⁷).

3²⁵. '*from our youth*'. The prophet may be indicating the time soon after the Lord had brought them out of Egypt (cf. 2¹).

4¹. '*if thou wilt . . . unto me shalt thou return*'. Do not waste time talking about repentance: repent, and have done with it! Then you will no longer 'wander' like Cain (note *RV*m, and cf. *RV*m of Gen 4¹⁶).

4². '*the nations shall bless themselves in him*'. See Genesis 18¹⁸, 22¹⁸, 26⁴, 48²⁰.

It is possible to feel sorry for the punishment that disloyalty brings, without feeling any sorrow for the disloyalty itself. That is why, even when sins are coming home to roost, there may be the need for someone to speak the word of the Lord, to declare His promise and command—'Be converted'. This is Jeremiah's task. Judah has learned nothing from history. She has seen the northern kingdom punished for disloyalty by being divorced from the Lord and destroyed (3^8), yet although there was a time when she pretended that she was taking a different attitude (3^{10}), she is even worse than the northern kingdom. Judah too must suffer, but that will not be the end. When Judah has been taught how worthless are the gods on whom she has squandered so much that is precious (3^{23-4}), the time will come when the Lord will bring Israel and Judah together back into the promised land (3^{18}). It is still the purpose of the Lord to make His people the means of His 'salvation unto the end of the earth' (Isa 49^6). But first His people must repent (4^1), '*with her whole heart*' and not '*feignedly*' (3^{10}).

An important word here is '*return*' ($3^{7, 10, 12, 14, 22}$, 4^1). It stands for an 'about turn', a complete reversal of attitude, an abandoning of '*treacherous*' rebellion against a Sovereign Lord ($3^{7, 8, 10, 20}$), for a complete acceptance of His authority. It means turning right away from 'Our will be done by Thee' to the way of life which is based on 'Thy will be done by us'. It means ceasing to use religion as a method of buying what we desire, and becoming willing to be used by God to bring about what He desires. It means abandoning ways of thinking and habits of behaviour which aim at self-satisfaction, and allowing one's life to be spent in satisfying the Lord, in obeying the voice of the living God ($3^{13, 17, 25}$) whose word is '*truth*', '*judgement*' and '*righteousness*' (4^2).

It is because Jeremiah insists on a clearer understanding of the nature of sin that he is able to point also to a deeper understanding of the meaning of repentance. God is '*merciful*' (3^{12}); His activity shows that He is faithful and trustworthy. That is where everything begins; that is the sole reason why repentance is possible. This is the Love that never fails. Only *because* 'the kingdom of God is at hand' is it possible to 'repent' and 'believe in the gospel' (Mk 1^{15}). Only God's *chesed*, His steadfast love which goes even to the Cross for us, can show us how far we are gone in our turning away from Him, and how great is our guilt. Only God's *chesed* can give us also the assurance that our deadness to His touch (3^{17} and cf. Eph 4^{18}) can be dealt with effectively; that our '*heart*' can be changed (cf. $3^{10, 15, 17}$) so that our whole personality is turned round to move willingly, steadily and energetically back to God (cf. Hos 12^7).

> *He who all your lives hath strove,*
> *Wooed you to embrace His love;*
> *Will you not His grace receive?*
> *Will you still refuse to live?*   (*MHB* 327)

> *Thou knowest the way to bring me back,*
>   *My fallen spirit to restore:*
> *O for Thy truth and mercy's sake,*
>   *Forgive, and bid me sin no more . . .*   (*MHB* 346)

We must acknowledge our sin, sorrow for it, and continue to have faith in the sure, trustworthy Love that has brought us back. Genuine repentance is always a response to the God whose call comes to us while we are yet sinners (cf. **31¹⁸**). It is very different from a paralysing remorse; it is a return to the Source of every kind of blessedness. To Him we may, we can, we must return (cf. **4¹⁻²**).

There is further important material on repentance in the next section (**4³⁻⁴**).

4³⁻⁴: Judah, repent!

An urgent warning is given to Judah that the Lord will bring destruction upon her unless there is complete repentance.

4³. '*Break up . . . thorns*'. The '*fallow ground*' has to lose its hardness and be cleaned of weeds if it is ever to produce good fruit (cf. Hos 10¹²).

4⁴. '*Circumcise . . . heart*'. The metaphor changes, and now it is the '*heart*' that needs to be cleansed and devoted to the Lord (cf. Deut 10¹⁶, 30⁶, Col 2¹¹). The uncircumcised heart is closed to the Lord, just as the uncircumcised ear (**6¹⁰**) is closed to His word.

Both the metaphors used here assert the need for, and the possibility of, conversion. Judah is like uncultivated land that is foul with weeds and is baked hard; she is a people whose heart needs to have the Lord's mark set upon it. Circumcision means that a descendant of Abraham is dedicated to the Lord and owes his whole loyalty to Him, and Jeremiah longs to see God's stamp set upon the '*heart*' of His people, that is on

their thoughts, their will, their whole personality. The prophet
knows that his people will have to undergo the same purging
process that he is himself experiencing (cf. **4**¹⁴, **15**¹⁹, **17**⁹, **31**³³).
If the '*fire*' (verse 4) of God's love is not allowed to do its
refining, cleansing work, then it must do a work of destruction
in them.

In his own experience Jeremiah knows that any repentance
which is a genuine turning to the Lord is far from being a light
thing; the 'refining fire' must 'go through' the heart and
'sanctify the whole' (*MHB* 387). He also recognizes that
circumcision   is   valueless   unless   the   outward   sign   is
accompanied by inward grace (cf. **9**²⁶). Paul says that 'we are
the circumcision' (Phil 3³); we are those who have received
God's covenant, the New Covenant in the blood of Jesus,
those who are offering ourselves to God as a living sacrifice
(Rom 12¹). 'For he is not a Jew which is one outwardly . . .
and circumcision is that of the heart' (Rom 2²⁸⁻⁹). It is still
possible for us to observe all the regulations that apply to us
as members of the Church, but to refuse to let God deal with
the 'heart', to refuse to allow His grace to make us work out
our own salvation according to His perfect will. Jeremiah
tells us that that way lies disaster. However venerable the
rules and the traditions and the customs may be, they have not
fulfilled their purpose unless they are providing the conditions
in which we are being given

> *A heart resigned, submissive, meek,*
> *My great Redeemer's throne . . .*
> *A heart in every thought renewed,*
> *And full of love divine.*   (*MHB* 550)

4⁵⁻³¹: Chaos is come again

A horn sounds the alarm and a watchman shrieks a warning
as the enemy gathers, advances and attacks. The prophet has
a vision of chaos, and of panic and flight. He hears the death-
cry of Jerusalem. His heart is bursting with compassion because
God's people, blind to this approaching terror, are stupidly
persisting in their evil ways.

4⁵. '*trumpet*'. The horn sounded by the watchman when the enemy was sighted, to call people inside the fortifications (cf. **4**¹⁹, Amos 3⁶, Joel 2¹).

'*fenced cities*'. Towns with fortifications.

4⁶. '*standard*'. A mast or pole to which the men could rally.

'*the north*'. See the commentary on 1¹³⁻¹⁴. In a vision such as this it is unlikely that the poet was concerned to identify the exact nationality of the foe.

4¹⁰. '*Then said I*'. As *LXX* indicates, this should probably be 'They say' or 'They shall say'.

'*reacheth unto the soul*'. Better, as in *RSV*, 'reached their very life'.

4¹². '*a full wind . . .*'. What is meant is 'a wind too strong for winnowing' (cf. *RV*m), a stiff breeze that would carry the grain away as well as the chaff. The point is that no discrimination will be made between those whose offences are heavy and those whose offences are light. All have sinned. Cf. **5⁵**.

4¹³. '*as clouds*'. The speed of a rain cloud moving across the sub-tropical sky, especially in the dry season, has to be seen to be believed.

4¹⁵. '*Dan*', '*Ephraim*'. Both are to the north (cf. verse 6). Again the suggestion is of an irresistibly swift advance, since Dan is seventy miles from Ephraim.

4¹⁶. '*a far country*'. The poet hints again at a mysterious enemy; see commentary on verse 6.

4¹⁷. '*As keepers of a field*'. The meaning seems to be that the besieging troops, the '*watchers*' of verse 16, are encircling a Judah which is as defenceless as an open field. Fields were not enclosed with fences or walls in Jeremiah's day.

4¹⁹. '*bowels*'. Because strong feelings of fear and anxiety and excitement often affect the digestion, this part of the body was believed to be the organ with which one experienced strong emotion. *RSV* paraphrases, 'My anguish, my anguish!'.

'*the alarm of war*'. The battle-cry.

4²⁰. Cf. **10²⁰.**

4²³. Cf. Genesis 1².

4²⁷. This verse in prose interrupts the poem and may be a later addition made by a scribe who felt that things were going too far. It may be based on **5¹⁰, ¹⁸, 30¹¹.**

4²⁸. '*not repented*'. The Lord has not 'changed His mind'.

4³⁰. '*enlargest thine eyes with paint*'. Cf. 2 Kings 9³⁰. Though she dresses smartly and uses the most skilful make-up and attractive accessories, Judah will have no appeal for those who have now turned against her, her former allies and '*lovers*'. Cf. **13²¹.**

We are dealing here with splendid vivid poetry, born out of the pity, fear, indignation and sense of urgency of a man who deeply loved his country. The prophet tries, with all the skill and eloquence that he can command, to confront his people with a picture of what could be the consequence of their settled habit of disloyalty to the Lord. Inescapable trouble is coming to destroy the whole nation. It will be like a lion (verse 7); like a fierce, hot wind from the desert which is too strong to winnow the less unworthy from the more (verses 11-12); like vultures swooping quickly on a carcase (this is probably the picture in verse 13; 'vultures' not '*eagles*'); like hunters encircling a doomed beast (verse 17). The result will be a chaos such as has never been seen since the universe was first created. The death-shriek of Judah will be like the cry of a woman giving birth with difficulty to her first child. Her political and religious leaders will be dazed and stupefied; they will blame the Lord because He has not fulfilled the fair promises of the false prophets (verses 9-10). The people will suffer because they are stupid ('*sottish*') and do not '*know*' the Lord in the only way in which He is to be known, which is the keeping of His covenant (verse 22). God is consistent; He will not change His mind (cf. verse 28). Therefore Jeremiah must suffer in anticipation, with feelings that seem to burst the walls of his heart (cf. *RV*m of verse 19). Yet all the sincerity and power of his urgent pleading seem to have no effect.

Judah is determined to keep moving towards the crash that will be her end (verse 14).

The Lord has done everything possible to turn Judah, to lead her to repent. Now He must bring devastation upon her by means of a foe whom she cannot seduce (verse 30). The leaders who have lulled the people into a false sense of security will be the first to fail when this enemy strikes, though they will still be ready to blame the Lord rather than admit that it is their bad leadership which is at fault (verses 9-10). Like Amos long before him, Jeremiah sees that the Day of the Lord is to be a day of wrath for God's own people. This word of judgement affects him deeply. He is one with his people, and yet he is not of them since he is God's prophet. (Notice 'us' in verse 8, and cf. Phil 3[18] where it is 'with tears' that Paul speaks of those who are 'heading for destruction' (*NEB*). So also Jesus grieved, but still could offer no hope to the impenitent; cf. Lk 19[41-4].)

In the remarkable poem in verses 23-5 we have what might almost be the thoughts of the last man left on earth as he surveys the effects of nuclear weapons (cf. Ps 102[25-6], Isa 24[19-20], 34[11], Heb 12[26-7]). The atmosphere might be that of Nevil Shute's novel *On the Beach*, or of the film based on it. But Jeremiah is less concerned with the details of the ruin to come than with the Lord who sends it and can use it for His righteousness and His salvation. The prophet knows something of the cost to God of His coming in righteousness and salvation. It is the false prophets who have no fellowship in the suffering of God, but Jeremiah is not of their company and he cannot escape (cf. verses 9-10).

Preachers are perhaps not reluctant to speak about the perils of nuclear war, about the sins of bad leaders, or even about the ingenuity in doing evil of those people who seem to be ignorant of how '*to do good*' (verse 22). But we notice also that a true prophet is himself affected first, and even most, by the message that God gives him to deliver, and he is one with his people in their sufferings. It is the false prophet who has no share in the sufferings of God as He deals with His own people. (Notice verses 8 and 19. Cf. Isa 65[2], Rom 10[1], Phil 3[18], Acts 20[31].) There is a story of how, when a vital cable snapped during a broadcast by King George V, a young engineer held the two ends together, enduring the electric shocks so that the King's message could go through. So a preacher may be shaken, but the King's word has to get through to His people. Pain battered Jeremiah's heart, even as the enemy is going to batter the walls of the towns of Judah. Do these things account for any of the difference between what our preaching is and what it ought to be, for any of the differences between what the witness of the Church is and what it ought to be?

We notice also how Jeremiah's understanding of the nature of sin and his shrinking from the bitter consequences that must come upon those who forsake God (verses 17, 18, and 22) lead him to insist that the '*heart*' must be washed clean (verse 14). It is only because God will create a *new* heart that there is sure hope that, even if chaos has first to return, there will be a new creation (cf. 31³¹⁻⁶, Isa 54¹⁰). Because God is faithful, even a death-shriek may be the cry heralding a new birth (cf. verse 31).

5¹⁻⁶: Not one just man

Jeremiah searches Jerusalem for one just man, first among the poor, then among the great. But in vain. This is why punishment is bound to fall upon the city.

5³. '*return*'. Better 'repent' (cf. *RSV*).

5⁴. '*judgement*'. This is *mishpat*, decision by custom, case law based on precedent (cf. 8⁷, where the word is translated '*ordinance*' while the margin has 'judgement'). Here it is parallel to '*the way*': it is the way that the Lord teaches to those who walk with Him. Cf. *NHS* pp. 74-6.

5⁶. Read 'a wolf from the desert shall kill them'.

What the Lord requires is loyalty, 'faithfulness' (*RV*m of verse 1). This bears fruit in righteous conduct, and God's discipline works to produce it (verse 3). But the people will not learn. Even those who are accounted '*great*' behave like oxen who break loose from the '*yoke*' that links them to the plough, and then run wild (verse 5). So they become easy prey for the wild beasts (verse 6).

There is a considerable difference between this section and

the dialogue between Abraham and the Lord in Genesis 18²³⁻³³. Here the search is undertaken on God's orders because it is His desire to '*pardon*' (verse 1). But the prophet cannot find anyone who is seeking '*the truth*'; there is no man who is following God's way, the way that He makes plain in all His dealings with His people. Jeremiah is like a lone lookout on a ship who has seen icebergs ahead, but who cannot make either the officers or the crew take notice of his warning (cf. verse 3).

Notice that to 'do justly' and to 'seek truth' are inseparable aspects of the same way of life. This is because '*truth*' (verse 1), here and elsewhere in the Bible, is what is trustworthy and reliable, even as the Lord is trustworthy and reliable. The man who seeks this 'truth' is the man who acts justly; he can be relied on because he himself is relying upon God. At each stage of his pilgrim's progress he has the fellowship and protection of One who is absolutely dependable and who knows every step of the way (cf. Ps 1⁶). This truth which we are to seek is also 'faithfulness' (see *RV*m of verses 1 and 3, also Deut 32⁴, Ps 33⁴, 36⁵). It is something to be done (cf. Jn 3²¹, 1 Jn 1⁶); it is something to be obeyed (cf. Gal 5⁷, 1 Pet 1²²). The whole of life can be worship in truth (Jn 4²³), if we know the way of, and keep company with, the One who is 'the way, and the truth, and the life'.

> *Jesu, my Truth, my Way,*
> *My sure, unerring Light . . .*
> *Teach me the happy art*
> *In all things to depend*
> *On Thee; O never, Lord, depart,*
> *But love me to the end!*   (*MHB* 635)

'Amen' is from the same root as the word translated '*truth*' in verse 1. When we say 'Amen' we are, or should be, affirming our faith in God who is utterly reliable; we are committing ourselves to show complete reliability in our own lives as we walk '*in the way of the Lord*'. 'It is through Christ Jesus that we say "Amen"' (2 Cor 1²⁰ in *NEB*), and the gospel for a world riddled with distrust is that He is 'the Amen, the faithful and true witness, the beginning of the creation of God' (Rev 3¹⁴). Even in days when '*transgressions are many*' and '*backslidings are increased*', when the '*poor*' are '*foolish*' and the '*great*' have '*broken the yoke*' (verses 4-6), He goes on searching for those who seek truth, and they will surely meet.

5⁷⁻¹⁹: Darkness at noon

Israel and Judah are completely disloyal to God, despite all that He has done, and a foreign invader will devour them.

5¹⁰. '*walls*'. Better 'vine rows' (cf. *RSV*).

5¹⁷. '*which thy sons and they daughters should eat*'. Follow *RSV* here: 'they shall eat up your sons and your daughters'.
    '*fenced cities*'. Strongholds (cf. 34⁷).

God's people are rebels: this is clear from the way in which they behave and the way in which they honour false gods. The prosperity that the Lord granted to them has not evoked gratitude and obedient service, but has been met with corrupt apostasy (verse 7). The Lord's vineyard (see comment on verse 10 and cf. 2²¹) is to be destroyed, because His messengers have been treated with contempt. Their warnings have been ignored as if they were nothing but hot air (cf. verse 13). God's word is no empty breath: it is a destroying flame (verse 14). Jeremiah is still not anxious to identify the nation that God will use to punish His rebel people (verse 15, cf. Deut 28³³, ⁴⁹⁻⁵³). It is sufficient for his purpose that they will speak a language that the men of Judah do not understand. Their arrows will fly so swiftly that their quivers become empty with the emptiness of death (verse 16). So the punishment will fit the crime: those who chose to serve foreign gods while they were in their own land will be made to serve foreign masters in exile (verse 19).

The mood of 'It can't happen here' (verse 12, cf. Zeph. 1¹²) arises from 'practical atheism', the attitude which is summed up in 5², the way of life which ignores the fact that we have a Lord (cf. Ps 14¹, Isa 56⁹⁻¹²). Against such complacency God's word is a searing fire (cf. 23²⁹). The prophets from Amos onwards warned the optimists who believed that God must see to the welfare of His people, no matter how they behaved, that they would find out to their cost that they were wrong. It is argued in some places in our day that the 'concept of God', however useful it may once have been, must be discarded by those who have any claim to 'psychological maturity'. But even more common is the 'practical atheism' of those who perhaps pay lip-service to God, but live as if He can be ignored for all practical purposes. There is also the attitude—'Keep religion out of politics, out of business, etc.'. Those who say, in so many different ways, '*It is not he*' (verse 12) still need to be warned that this attitude can lead only to disaster. There is no 'Do-it-yourself Kit' that can help men to abundant life: it needs all the energy of God, manifested in the birth and death and resurrection of His Son, to bring us to such maturity. The '*God of hosts*' (verse 14) still rules the universe, and those who will not let Him make Himself known in times of prosperity must be prepared to find that He is making Himself known through disaster (cf. Lk 12¹³⁻²¹).

5²⁰⁻³¹: A shoreless sea of evil

Although God is the Controller of all the mighty forces of nature, His people do not fear Him and there is no limit to their wickedness.

5²⁰. '*Declare ye*'. Here it is the people who are instructed to declare the word of the Lord (cf. 4⁵).

5²¹. '*understanding*'. The 'heart' (*RV*m) was regarded as the seat of whatever side of a man's nature might be uppermost at any particular time; it might be his '*understanding*' or his will or his good sense. The point here seems to be that they are lacking in sense (cf. *RSV*).

5²⁴. '*rain . . . in its season*'. New Year came in September with the harvest full moon, so that the '*former*' rain came in October and '*the latter*' in March or April. We should speak of the beginning and end of the rainy season (cf. 3³).

5²⁷. '*cage*'. Better 'basket'. The picture is of a crate of birds in the market.

5²⁸. '*they shine*'. They are sleek.
'*they overpass*'. They recognize no limits.

5²⁹. Cf. verse 9 and 9⁹.

5³¹. '*by their means*'. Many of the prophets appear to have been associated with the shrines and to have worked with the priests, perhaps giving them help in matters where the Law seemed to offer no explicit guidance. It is hard to believe that such prophets as Jeremiah were linked with the shrines in this way, though some scholars have tried to maintain that all Hebrew prophets fall into this pattern.

God is in control of everything: if only men would recognize this, they would be bound to honour Him (verse 22). Cf. Ps 104⁹, Job 38⁸, Rom 1²⁰⁻¹. He rules even the mighty seas and prevents the waters from overwhelming the earth and bringing back chaos. He it is, and not the *baalim*, who gives or withholds the life-giving rain. But the Lord's people will not see this. They follow easygoing preachers and leaders who are never likely to upset them by indicating that there is an '*end*' to the way of thinking and behaving that they have adopted (verse 31). They are rebels against their Creator, the Maker of heaven and earth, and 'the revolting heart will produce a revolting life' (Matthew Henry's comment on verse 23). God's sun and rain are for the just and the unjust, but there may come a time when they are withdrawn as a warning to the unjust, and as a reminder that sin blocks the stream of God's goodness towards us (verses 24-25 and cf. 3³).

Like other Hebrew prophets, Jeremiah is keenly aware of the connection between a wrong relationship to God and a wrong relationship to men (verses 23–8; cf. 34¹⁶⁻¹⁷). Only when a man worships God with his whole self is he able to love his neighbour as himself. There is little neighbourly love among the people of Judah; swindling and exploitation have become like a sport there (verse 26). It is an appalling and a disgusting thing (verse 30), but every group seems to like it so—'the world wills to belong to the Devil' (Luther). When they cease to fear God, men become blind and deaf, foolish and perverse, morally paralysed (verses 21-2). But their punishment is implicit in their conduct (verse 25 and cf. 6¹⁹). The God who is in control of everything is alert (cf. 1¹²); he sets a limit, which the power of evil can no more overleap than the sea can break its bounds.

As we learn more of the wonders of the structure of matter and begin to explore the trackless spaces of the universe, we must learn to honour our Creator, the Lord who has appointed an *'end'* for all things. To ignore Him is to be in the perilous state of being turned away from the only life that matters. God is always at work to save us from this folly; even a famine may be His way of leading us to repent. The trouble is always in the *'heart'*: that is the headquarters of the rebellion against Him. The God who is in control of everything can deal even with that. There lies our only hope when we are faced with the 64,000 dollar question, *'What will ye do in the end thereof?'* (verse 31). It is clear that we should attend to what the prophet has to say about the *'heart'*. See for example 4⁴, 7²⁴, 17⁹, 18¹², 23¹⁷, 31³³. A concordance will guide us further, and there is useful matter in *TWB*, p. 145.

6¹⁻¹⁵: Shaming the shameless

Jerusalem is a city where evil keeps on gushing out. The prophet is tired of trying to win a hearing there. Everyone rejects the word of the Lord and is therefore blind to the approaching disaster.

6¹. *'signal'*. Perhaps a smoke signal on a hill. Beacons were lit on many hills in England at the time of the threatened invasion by the Spanish Amarda.

'Beth-haccherem'. The modern Ain Krim, six miles west of Jerusalem. *'Tekoa'* is to the south of Jerusalem (cf. Amos 1¹).

6³. *'shepherds'*. Foreign rulers with their armies or *'flocks'*. See comment on 2⁸ (cf. 12¹⁰; Mic 5⁵).

6⁴. *'Prepare'*. Notice the margin—'sanctify'. Warriors were expected to be in a state of ritual cleanness (cf. 22⁷, Isa 13³, Deut 20², Ezek 21²¹⁻³).

'at noon'. The drowsy part of the day, a good time for a surprise attack.

'Woe unto us . . . stretched out'. Who is speaking is not clear, whether attackers or attacked. The remark may even be a comment by a scribe which has found its way from the margin into the text. Punctuation in the *RSV* indicates that

D

the speakers are different from those in the first half of this verse and in verse 5.

6⁵. '*by night*'. Also a time for surprise attack.

6⁶. '*trees*'. These could be used as battering rams, as well as for the construction of a siege-mound ('*mount*') from which arrows and other missiles could be shot over the walls.

'*she is wholly oppression in the midst of her.*' Read, 'she is corrupt through and through'.

6⁷. Follow *RV*m.

6⁸. '*lest my soul be alienated*'. Better 'lest I wrench myself away from you'.

6⁹. Follow *RV*m. The idea is of someone gleaning carefully so that not a single fruit is left on the stems; cf. '*throughly glean*'.

6¹⁰. '*To whom shall I speak*'. The prophet has now turned to his own difficulty (cf. **4⁴**).

6¹¹. '*Pour it out*'. For the cup of the Lord's fury, see comment on **25¹⁵**.

6¹². '*shall be turned unto*'. Better 'shall be handed over to'.

6¹⁴. See **28⁹** (cf. Ezek 13¹⁰).

Jerusalem is rotten to the core (verses 6, 13); she is a bubbling spring of wickedness from which fresh devilries go on gushing (verse 7). Evil and destruction are looming up from the menacing '*north*' (verse 1); disaster is so nearly certain that sensible people would already have left the capital for the comparative safety of nearby towns. At this late hour the Lord still pleads with '*the daughter of Zion*'. For Him to allow '*the comely and delicate one*' to be laid waste is tantamount to submitting Himself to a painful amputation (verse 8). But there is no alternative: she will not be '*instructed*'. This is evident, otherwise she would already be *carrying out* His instructions.

The search for one just man had failed (5¹⁻⁵), but now the prophet is told to try again; (notice '*thine*' in the second half of verse 9). Like a gleaner, he searches desperately for one good grape on the Lord's degenerate Vine (cf. 2²¹). But there is no-one whose '*ear*' is open to the word of the Lord (verse 10, cf. Acts 7⁵¹); again it seems that the '*least*' and the '*greatest*' are alike in this (verse 13, cf. 5⁴⁻⁵). The symptoms of this deafness to the word of God are (*a*) '*covetousness*' (verse 13), the violent self-assertion which is a form of idolatry (cf. Eph 5⁵, Col 3⁵); (*b*) unjustified optimism (verse 14 and cf. commentary on 5⁷⁻¹⁹): (*c*) shamelessness (verse 15). While such things exist, there can be no fellowship in the covenant with the Lord, and therefore there can be no '*peace*'. The prophet finds the tension unbearable (verse 11); people will not listen to him. They listen instead to those priests and prophets who allow them to keep their self-respect by prescribing palliative drugs, when it ought to be obvious that the celestial Surgeon alone can deal effectively with their disease (verse 14).

God's '*fury*' (verse 11) is the implacable hatred of sin which is an integral part of His love for us. It is wrong for preachers to suggest that the OT is less 'sophisticated' or 'humanitarian' in this matter than the NT. The suffering and dereliction and death of Jesus are the supreme demonstration of the truth that God's wrath falls on all the ungodliness of men (cf. Mk 15³⁴, Rev 19¹³⁻¹⁵, 2 Cor 5²¹). We all have good cause to fear God's wrath (Rom 2⁸⁻¹¹, Mt 10²⁸, Rev 6¹⁶). Whenever Christ crucified is preached, men are passing judgement on themselves. But where He is accepted, where men are being perfected in love, there they can be confident that God has not appointed us for wrath, but for 'the full attainment of salvation' (1 Thess 5⁹ in *NEB*: cf. 1 Jn 4¹⁷, Rom 8¹).

The Christian preacher should therefore know where true peace is to be found. He has no excuse for saying '*peace, peace; when there is no peace*' (verse 14). The Bible speaks of a positive peace which is far more than the absence of conflict, the peace that God gives when His judgement has done its work. So long as there is disregard of the Lord, and disloyalty to Him, there can be no peace (cf. 16⁵, 29¹¹, 33⁸⁻⁹). The peace which means fellowship, that harmony with God and our fellows in which alone we shall find true satisfaction, is a gift which can only come from the Lord (cf. *RV*m of Judg 6²⁴; also Isa 45⁷). In

society as well as in creation, He alone can overcome discord
and chaos. There can be no peace where men are not in a right
relationship with Him, since peace can exist only with
righteousness and truth (Isa 54¹³⁻¹⁴, 60¹⁷). It is useless to look
for peace where there is no peace: 'in the world you will have
trouble'. But there is a peace 'such as the world cannot give'
and Jesus Himself says, 'I have told you all this so that in me
you may find peace' (cf. Jn 14²⁷, 16³³ in *NEB*). It is because
this 'peace' is at stake that false prophets have to be attacked.
There can be no trifling with inadequate estimates of the
seriousness of sin, no diminution of the costliness of repentance;
the only way to the harmony of all things in heaven and on
earth, which is our true wellbeing, is by our Lord Jesus Christ
(see *TWB*, 165-6).

6¹⁶⁻²⁶: The wages of sin

The Lord tells the whole earth that His people must be
punished because they have persistently refused to walk in
the good way.

6¹⁶. '*the good way*'. Literally 'the way to the good' (cf. Mt
7¹³⁻¹⁴).

6¹⁷. '*watchmen*'. The prophets (cf. Ezek 3¹⁷).

6²⁰. '*sweet cane*'. This was used in the preparation of incense
(cf. **41⁵**; Ex 30²³).

6²². '*from the north country*'. See comment on 1¹³⁻¹⁴; cf.
50⁴¹⁻⁴³.

6²⁵. '*the way*'. The track across open country—'*the field*'
(cf. comment on 4¹⁷).

6²⁶. '*wallow thyself*'. *RSV* has 'roll in ashes'. (Cf. Ezek 27³⁰,
Isa 58⁵.)

God had provided His people with a 'way to the good', a way
that is trodden in every age by those who accept the 'yoke' of
the Kingdom, and so find 'rest' for their 'souls' (verse 16 and
cf. 2²⁻³). Once that 'way' has been abandoned, even the most

costly new forms of worship can provide no substitute for
it; all that God requires is obedience to His '*words*' and His
'*law*' (verses 19-20 and cf. 7²¹⁻³). But the people of Judah
refuse to go back to the crossroads (verse 16), they will not
return to the fork in the path and resume the right way, and
therefore an enemy is coming to destroy them (verse 26).

Progress which is not along the right path must lead to disaster,
and the swifter it is, the sooner disaster comes. There is a great
cloud of witnesses who '*show the same path to heaven*' (*MHB*
831), and that is the path we are to follow, '*the good way*'
(verse 16). In Bunyan's *Pilgrim's Progress* Goodwill tells Christian, 'That is the way thou must go: it was cast up by the
Patriarchs, Prophets, Christ and His Apostles; and it is straight
as a rule could make it'. It may be, as Jeremiah found, a
way where 'men love thee, heed thee, praise thee not', but it is
'the way the Master went'. Our generation badly needs non-
conformists; people who are not concerned with 'keeping
up with the Joneses', but with getting back to and following
'*the good way*'.

   The '*fruit of their thought*' (verse 19) should remind us that
wrong ideas, wrong habits of thinking, may yield a dreadful
harvest. 'Every human thought' has to 'surrender in obedience
to Christ' (*NEB* of 2 Cor 10⁵), and exotic types of devotion,
costly offerings from *Sheba* in Arabia and the '*far country*'
of India are no substitute for this (verse 20, cf. Prov 4²³).
When men cease to listen to God (verse 19), their worship
ceases to be the outward and visible sign of an inward and
spiritual fellowship; if they refuse to attend to the word of the
Lord, the ritual which ought to be an expression of repentance
and a signpost to a Saviour who is worthy of their trust,
becomes instead an insult to Him (cf. 18¹³⁻¹⁶, 7¹-8³).

6²⁷⁻³⁰: Refining fire

God's people are base metal that cannot be refined and so
must be thrown away.

6²⁷. '*a tower and a fortress*'. This is misleading,—see *RV*m.
RSV has 'I have made you an assayer and tester'. That is the
point; God sends the prophet to discover what sort of metal
His people are (cf. 9⁷, Ezek 22¹⁷⁻²², Mal 3²⁻³).

6²⁹. '*the lead*'. This was added so that it might remove impurities from the metal, but in this case it fails so that '*the wicked are not plucked away*'.

God's people are base metal. It might be expected that there is at least a small amount of good silver left in with the rest, but the most careful refining does not produce any. When lead is added, so that the silver may be separated and the alloys drawn away, it is found that there is no silver. They are all base metal. Hence 'silver rejects they are called because the Lord has rejected them' (verse 30).

This is yet another way of saying that there is not a single righteous man, not one good grape in all Judah (cf. **5¹⁻⁵**, **6⁹ᵇ**). God has known and tried their way, but every single one of them has turned to his own way. 'They are all stubbornly rebellious' (*RSV* of verse 28). It is no light thing to pray that the 'refining fire' might 'go through's one's heart' (*MHB* 387); would there in fact be anything left if it did? (Cf. Mt 3¹¹⁻¹².)

7¹-8³: How not to use the Lord's House

Jeremiah is sent to the Temple gate to proclaim that the Temple can give no security whatever to people who are disobedient to the Lord.

After the poetry of chapters **2-6** we now have this chapter in prose. There is another account of the same incident in chapter **26** where it is dated shortly after the death of Josiah at Megiddo (**26¹**).

7⁶. '*stranger*'. A resident alien.

7¹⁰. '*called by my name*'. The Lord appointed the Temple as a place where men were permitted to seek Him and discern His will in a special way. This house is so intimately connected with Him that to desecrate it is to insult the Lord Himself.

7¹². '*Shiloh*'. The ruins were not far from Anathoth. There is some archaeological evidence that it was destroyed, probably by the Philistines, about 1050 B C. Jeremiah was probably a descendant of the priests of Shiloh and he was well aware that it had once been an important centre of worship where the Ark was kept (cf. **26⁶**; Ps 78⁶⁰).

7¹⁸. '*the queen of heaven*'. Here is evidence of an open return to idolatry after the death of Josiah, cf. **44¹⁷**. The word translated '*cakes*' is borrowed by the Hebrew from the Babylonian. The '*queen of heaven*' was Anath, the goddess of love and fertility. She has so many features in common with Ishtar (Astarte) and with Asherah that it is difficult not to confuse them. It seems likely that, in Judah, Anath was popularly regarded as the wife of the Lord ('Yahweh'), a belief that was also to be found in later times among Jews settled at Elephantine in Egypt. Anathoth means 'the Anaths', so that Jeremiah's own town was named after her. Goddesses of this type received great attention because they were responsible for the increase of crops and the fertility of cattle.

In Assyria 'Ishtar' (connected with the planet Venus) was regarded as the mother of the gods and 'the mistress of the heavens and the stars'. To this day the most impressive sight in the excavated ruins of Babylon is the 'Gate of Ishtar', which Nebuchadrezzar had once decorated with gay enamelled reliefs of animals. In the Ras Shamra literature she appears frequently, sometimes as 'Astarte-name-of-Baal', and there is mention there also of 'the Virgin-Anath' who intercedes on behalf of the gods with the high god—'El'. (There is an illustration of Astarte plaques on p. 107 of Albright's *Archaeology of Palestine* (Pelican). See also *PH* (3), p. 171.)

7²¹. '*eat ye flesh*'. Whereas the worshippers received a share of the meat when there was a '*sacrifice*', this did not happen when there was a '*burnt offering*', as this was given in its entirety to God. But their whole attitude to God is wrong and that makes any type of sacrifice pointless, so they might just as well eat their 'burnt offerings', instead of letting them go up in smoke. It is as if the Lord says, 'Go ahead and eat the whole lot. Eat what you think is Mine as well as what you think is yours, because I do not want any of it.'

7²². '*your fathers*'. The reference is to the covenant which constituted Israel as God's people (cf. Amos 5²⁵, Hos 6⁶, Mic 6⁶⁻⁸, Ps 50¹²⁻¹⁵, 51¹⁶⁻¹⁷, Mt 12 ⁶⁻⁷, 5²³⁻⁴).

7²⁹. '*Cut off thine hair*'. A mourning custom. Hair goes on growing for some time after death and so was believed to have life in itself and to be an appropriate gift to the dead.

'*O Jerusalem*'. These words are not in the Hebrew, as the italics in *RV* indicate. It is reasonable to suggest that the saying is addressed to the city, but it may be addressed to the nation, or even to the prophet himself.

7³⁰. '*abominations*'. They have dared to set up idols even in the Lord's Temple (cf. Ezek 8 ⁵⁻¹²).

7³¹. '*to burn their sons and their daughters*'. Even at this stage, centuries after Abraham, children were still being sacrificed! It seems that even quite early in the reign of Jehoiakim things were as bad as they had been in the days of Manasseh; all the work of Josiah and his henchmen for reform had been quickly undone (cf. **19⁵, 32³⁵**, 2 Kings 23 ³ ⁶⁻⁷).

'*the valley of the son of Hinnom*'. This notorious place, just outside Jerusalem, is the origin of the NT idea of 'Gehenna'.

7³². '*till there be*'. Follow *RV*m, 'because there shall be' no other place available.

7³³. '*fray*'. This means 'frighten' in modern English. No one will be alive to scare away scavenging birds or beasts; a Hebrew could imagine no worse fate than this.

8¹. '*bones*'. Like hair (see comment on **7²⁹**), these were considered to contain life, so that to destroy bones is to make a complete end of someone.

8². '*they shall not be . . . buried*'. It was thought that anyone left unburied would never find rest—another feature of this picture of a horrible end.

The only source of security is the Lord, and He is one who must be obeyed (verses 5-6). It is ridiculous for His people to spend their days breaking the ten commandments (verse 9, cf. Mic 3¹¹) and yet still expect God to protect them. Ever since they entered the promised land they have gone from bad to worse, and they have now reached the point where they must be rejected. Jeremiah has no desire to see the holy city converted into a charnel house (7^{33}-8^3), but however great his grief may be, it is a small thing beside that of the Lord. God had willed that His people should remain '*in the land that I gave to your fathers for ever and ever*' (7^7, cf. 7^3, ^{5}, ^{25}). But they will not listen to His word; their sin is unto death, and Jeremiah is forbidden even to intercede for them (7^{16}, $^{26-7}$, cf. Mt 12^{31}).

Here we have a fine example of the courage of a man who is 'strong in the strength which God supplies'. One is reminded of Luther in the early stages of his battle against Rome. What Jeremiah is doing with amazing bravery is in flat contradiction of the settled conviction of princes, prophets, priests and people alike. They held that the source of security for the whole nation was the Temple and its sacrifices, and many of them would have quoted Isaiah in support of their conviction. Jeremiah is attacking their *religion* itself. He declares roundly that the sacrificial system was not asked for when they were given the Covenant and that it is not an essential part of God's way for His people (verse 22). Some scholars are inclined to write much more cautiously on this point, but this whole controversy hinges on the fact that Jeremiah plainly declared that the system of '*sacrifices*' and '*burnt offerings*' did not exist in the Wilderness. Whether the prophet was right or wrong, that is what he believed. (Incidentally a reasonable case *can* be made out for the view that the whole system was really Canaanite, as some of the Ras Shamra material may indicate.)

This incident marks one of the turning points of history. The Temple had been solemnly established as the sole place in the whole land for the sacrificial worship of the Lord only as recently as the reformation of Josiah. Now there comes a prophet who claims to speak in the name of the Lord, and he attacks the whole thing as if it were an idol! No wonder that he is regarded by everyone as a blasphemous iconoclast (cf. chapter 26). But if we regard the work that God did in Jeremiah as part of the shining Everest range of the OT, then we are here at the 'south summit' and there remains only the final ridge that leads to 31^{31-4} and to Isaiah 53.

In chapter 26 the main interest is the effect of delivering the message, and especially the way in which the prophet was affected: here in chapter 7 the interest is the content of the message itself. There must be an end of Temple and sacrifice, not because they are bad in themselves, but because the people of Judah are using them to their own harm. Temple and sacrifice must go, both of them, since they are being used in ways which deny the truth that their salvation lies only in the grace of God. Every prop must be knocked away so that God's people are able to see clearly that they depend entirely on their Lord. Only thus can real worship become possible (7³⁻¹¹; cf. Isa 1¹⁶). Their settled habits and isolated actions (the '*ways and doings*' of 7³), all must be changed radically so that they enjoy that true knowledge of God which is faithful obedience to Him.

Those who are treating the Temple as if it were '*a den of robbers*', a bandit headquarters where they can lie up safely between raids, must not be surprised if the Lord also 'regards it as such' (this seems to be the meaning of '*have seen it*' in 7¹¹). They cannot hope to remain in their own '*place*', the land of Judah (7³, ¹⁴, ²⁰). No shrine is sacrosanct if it gets in the way of the Lord's purpose; He showed that long ago at '*Shiloh*' (cf. 26⁶). The covenant does not centre on shrines, but on '*I will be your God, and ye shall be my people*', so that it cannot be '*well*' with them unless they '*walk*' in '*all the way*' that He commands (7²³; cf. 31³³, Amos 3¹⁻³). If they will not do that, it makes no matter how much else they may do, since the Lord will destroy not only His Temple but them also. His purposes will continue without them, since the One who has controlled events '*from of old*' is able to control them '*even for evermore*' (7⁷).

Our 'stewardship' only becomes 'Christian' when we recognize that the Lord has the disposal of our whole lives and not simply of our income. *Wesley's Hymns* included a section warning the religious about 'Formal Religion', and John Wesley in his *Journal* for 14th May, 1738, quotes with approval a letter which stated, 'I have seen . . . how intolerable the doctrine of faith is to the mind of man; and how peculiarly intolerable to religious men. . . . But this is not to be wondered at. For all religious people have such a quantity of righteousness, acquired by much painful exercise, and formed at last into current habits, which is their wealth, both for this world and the next. . . . But the doctrine of faith is a downright robber. It takes away all this wealth, and only tells us it is deposited for us with somebody else, upon whose bounty we must live like mere beggars.'

That again is the insight of Jeremiah; visibility can become poor precisely because of the smoke of sacrifice. We may use religion as a shelter where we hide from God's real requirements, and He may have to blow us out of it. Jesus tells us that we must love God and our neighbour before we can make a proper use of ritual, and the Cross clearly demonstrates that sacrifice is *God*'s action—

> *Christ the heavenly Lamb*
> *Takes all our sins away.* (*MHB* 234)

Acceptable offerings are always a sharing in this offering. The important thing about worship is not whether we have 'a good time' or 'feel better', not whether we 'like' the hymns or the prayers or the sermon, but whether God likes what we do; what He likes is thanksgiving in the name of His Son, from people whose lives are being spent in gratitude to Him. God is ready to allow all the churches and chapels and halls and cathedrals to go if they are used as a means of escape from the offering that He requires. Dearly loved buildings, familiar hymns and forms of service, traditions of every kind may become stumbling blocks if they are used as a substitute for the offering of ourselves as a living sacrifice, presented to God through Jesus Christ our Lord. Cf. the prayer beginning 'O Lord and heavenly Father, we Thy humble servants entirely desire Thy fatherly goodness. . . ' in the Communion Service.

We have (*a*) a Sacrifice and (*b*) a Temple. (*a*) The whole life of Jesus is His Sacrifice, and the Resurrection is God's manifest acceptance of this perfect offering. Jesus' startling command to drink His blood breaks through all the OT taboos about blood, and yet is their fulfilment. Because the blood *is* the life, and Jesus comes that we may have life in abundance, it is in His blood that the New Covenant is given. We are privileged to see what the prophets could only desire and long for, the kingdom of heaven open to all believers, because He overcame the sharpness of death. When we are in Him, and He in us, we share in the life of God in a way that the old Israel, with all its sacrifices, could never know. Jeremiah could see what was needed (cf. 31^{31-4}), but he could not see that God would make it possible through the Sacrifice of His Son. (Dr N. H. Snaith's *Mercy and Sacrifice* is valuable here.) (*b*) There can be, and is, but one Temple: Christ is the foundation and cornerstone of a Temple, not a thing of stones and mortar made with hands, but built of living men (cf. Isa 66$^{1-2,\ 20-1}$, Jn 1^{14}, 4$^{20-4}$, 1 Pet 2$^{4-10}$). Christ is the one in whom 'the whole building is bonded together' (*NEB* of Eph 2^{21}). The Church is not to be a '*den of robbers*' who are filching for themselves what belongs to God, but 'a house of prayer for all peoples' (Isa 56^7), a community that is continually growing into a holy temple in the Lord (Eph 2^{21}). Jesus is God-with-us, the Lord dwelling among men, the fulfilment of all that the Temple stands for. The dwelling of God among His people takes place through the Holy Spirit; Jesus has promised to be wherever two or three are met in His name. So we have a Temple. (In these paragraphs some ideas and phrases from my *The Old Testament in the Church* have been repeated. See especially pp. 80-7.)

This section of *Jeremiah* may also help us to be on our guard against the tendency to make the Lord's promise that 'the gates of Hades will not prevail' against His Church imply that the 'west' or 'democracy' must prevail also, and that God is bound to support us. We have no authority to try to sell Christianity as 'the bulwark of civilization', especially when our definition of civilization is 'our way of doing things'. The only civilization that will endure is that of people whose citizenship is in heaven. Real faith in God means that we are prepared to see the destruction, at His command, even of the very things which to us seem to be the only means of fulfilling His purpose (cf. the command to Abraham to sacrifice Isaac; our Lord going to the Cross).

Another jolt to our normal ways of thinking comes in 7^{16} (cf. 11^{14}). Are there limits to intercessory prayer? Part of Jeremiah's suffering here arises from the fact that he has been in the *habit* of interceding for his people, but now it seems that the Lord will no longer permit him to do so. Although God is patient and longs for men to repent (7$^{3,\ 25}$), there are some people who choose death rather than life. They will not listen to His word, and there comes the point where they seem to be past praying for (7$^{27-8}$). Intercession is not a simple thing (cf. **14^{11}**, **15^1**, 1 Sam 15^{29}, Isa 31$^{1-2}$, Mk 3$^{28-9}$, 1 Jn 5^{16}). We have no right to beg God to prolong a state of affairs that is more than ripe for judgement, any more than we have to ask Him to punish before the right time. It is all so difficult.

But it is our privilege to pray 'in the name of the Lord Jesus Christ'. We may have complete confidence in submitting all things to a Holy God, knowing that Jesus is always on His knees on behalf of sinners. If anything can be achieved it is by the prayer of Him who suffered and died for our sins.

If ever God forbids us to pray for anyone, He may also require us to tell them so. Jeremiah *makes it known* that he has been ordered not to intercede for them. May it not be that his speaking to them in this way is itself his prayer for them?

8^{4-13}: Nothing but withered leaves

Even the wild birds know their appointed way, but God's people persistently refuse to follow the way He has appointed for them. Scribes and wise men, prophets and priests, must all meet with heavy punishment because, instead of protesting, they themselves join in this flouting of the Lord's instructions.

8^5. *'they hold fast deceit'*. They cling tight to what is wrong.

8^7. *'turtle'*. This is of course the 'turtle-dove'; *'swallow'*—the Hebrew possibly means the bird we know as a 'swift'.

'ordinance'. This is *mishpat* (notice 'judgement' in *RV*m). See commentary on 5^4.

8^8. *'wrought falsely'*. Follow *RV*m (cf. 2 Chr 34^{13}).

8^{10-12}. These sentences occur also in 6^{12-15} which seems to be a more appropriate context.

8^{13}. *'the things that I have given them . . .'*. The Hebrew is obscure as *RV*m suggests. (For the first part of the verse, cf. Hab 3^{17-18}, Mt 21^{19}.)

The collection of sayings which starts in 8^4 continues to 9^{11}. In this first part of the collection the prophet points out that if a man is sensible he will get up again when he falls, and he will turn back if he mistakes the road. But Judah is not like that: she has fallen and will not get up; she has taken the wrong turning but will not turn back. God listens carefully for even one word of repentance, but His people are possessed

by a demon of apostasy (cf. **18¹³**) and they are going headlong
away from Him (verse 6). They claim to be '*wise*' and to have
'*the Law*' (verse 8), when in fact their attitude and behaviour
show that they are ignorant of God's teaching (verse 7).

Much more is known now about the migration of birds (verse
7) than was known in Jeremiah's day, but greater knowledge
makes this 'natural' behaviour and the way that it is 'built in'
to each bird seem more, rather than less, wonderful. But we
ought to feel still greater wonder that men will not follow
the good way that God appoints for them. Our heart is restless
until it finds its rest in Him, but still we refuse to go to Him.
It is all so unnatural; it goes in the face of the meaning of the
whole creation:

> *God, who did your being give,*
> *Made you with Himself to live;*
> *He the fatal cause demands,*
> *Asks the work of His own hands,*
> *Why, ye thankless creatures, why*
> *Will you cross His love, and die?* (*MHB* 327)

The ordinance (*mishpat*) of the Lord (verse 7) is the God-
appointed way which is made known by Him as He continues
to companion with His people. Migratory birds do what they
are created to do; they go and come back at the appropriate
time for their own wellbeing. Man was made to come to God:
the mystery is that he will not do what he is created for. He
prefers to behave as if he made himself: he cannot bear to
be reminded that there is anything superior to him in the
universe; that God is in heaven and he is on earth; that he
makes himself ridiculous by claiming the right to pass judgement on the word of his Lord instead of listening to Him
reverently and obeying. So when the Creator comes to this
part of His creation, looking for fruit to gather, He has to say,

> 'there are no grapes on the vine,
>   nor figs on the fig-tree;
> even the leaves are withered,
>   and what I gave them has passed away from them'
>   (**8¹³** in *RSV*).

Unless there is some radical change in the attitude of men to
God there can never be peace in God's creation. Jeremiah

knows that man needs a new heart. He cannot see *how* this can come about, but he trusts God to do it. His trust was not misplaced: the gospel is that, in Christ, God was reconciling the world to Himself. Therefore, if a man is in Christ, there *is* a new creation.

8¹⁴⁻¹⁷: Terror, not peace

The whole land will shake with terror when the Lord sends an implacable invader.

8¹⁴. Follow *RV*m (cf. **4⁵**).

8¹⁶. '*Dan*'. At the northern end of the old kingdom of Israel (cf. **4¹⁵**).

8¹⁷. Follow *RV*m, 'adders'.

False prophets led the people to expect '*peace*' and '*healing*' (verse 15), but now the people realize that God has decreed their ruin (verse 14). Preachers who are called to proclaim good news of 'peace by Jesus Christ' (Acts 10³⁶) know also that there is no peace except as the 'effect of righteousness' (Isa 32¹⁷ in *RSV*).

8¹⁸-9¹¹: The prophet's sorrow and the Lord's tears

Jeremiah longs to be far away from his own people, since their only progress is in evil.

8¹⁸. The Hebrew is uncertain here; see *RSV*.

8¹⁹. '*from a land that is very far off*'. *RV* and *AV* are both misleading here. Read 'from the length and breadth of the land' (of Judah) as in *RSV* (cf. Isa 33¹⁷).

8²⁰. '*The harvest is past, the summer is ended*'. Several commentators suggest that this is virtually a proverbial expression, and the assonance in the Hebrew gives some support to this view. Probably we should take the two phrases as parallel, so that the point of the saying is that the harvest (New Year) season has gone, and yet the change of fortune that one expects at such a time has not taken place. Other commentators see here a reference to *two* harvests: the wheat harvest in April-May and the grape harvest in July-September. But more probably the interpretation should depend, as suggested earlier, on the fact that everyone looked forward to a change of fortune at the New Year, which began for the Hebrews with an all-night celebration at the grape-harvest full moon. This time that change of fortune has *not* come.

8²². '*balm*'. The medicine was prepared from the resin of a tree which grew in '*Gilead*' across the Jordan (cf. Isa 1⁵⁻⁷).

9². '*a lodging place of wayfaring men*'. A traveller's rest-house, a caravanserai with only occasional passing visitors. The prophet is longing to be 'away from it all'.

9³. '*as it were their bow*'. Lies fly from their '*tongue*' like poison-tipped arrows.

9⁵⁻⁶. '*they weary themselves . . . they refuse to know me*'. As the *LXX* indicates, the text originally was something like 'they do evil and are too exhausted to repent. They pile oppression on oppression, and deceit on deceit; they refuse to know me.'

9⁷. '*melt . . . and try*'. Another reference to the smelting and refining of metal (cf. 6²⁷⁻³⁰).

9⁹. Cf. 5²⁹.

9¹⁰. '*pastures of the wilderness*'. These were the grazing areas used in the summer: now there are neither '*cattle*' nor even wild '*fowl*' or '*beast*' to be seen there.

The situation out of which this poem comes may be indicated in 2 Kings 24¹⁻². The '*I*' of 9¹⁰ may be the prophet or it may be the Lord (but cf. *RSV* where the *LXX* is followed). Whatever the correct translation may be, it is true that the devastation of Judah is a painful thing to the Lord. Here is a situation where 'this hurts me more than it hurts you' applies in all seriousness (cf. chapter **45**). God cannot be an impassive spectator of ruin, and neither can his prophet, whatever his own wishes may sometimes be (9¹⁻²). Though men sometimes think that God is not concerned about the sufferings of His people (cf. **14⁸**), He is in fact hurt, not only by their sin, but also by the suffering which is the consequence of sin (**8²¹**).

Jeremiah sees the old unregenerate 'Jacob' nature flourishing instead of the loyalty of Israel to the Lord ('*supplant*' in **9⁴** is an allusion to Jacob). Because the people '*refuse to know*' the Lord (**9⁶**) they are living demonstrations of every imaginable sin of the tongue—slander, deceit, lying, double-dealing (**9³⁻⁸**). But the night comes. . . . They are concerned to be '*saved*' from material disaster, but they are not interested in being 'saved' from all unrighteousness (**8²⁰**). The congregation of the faithful has degenerated into a congregation '*of treacherous men*' (**9²**), so the question that the Lord asks, '*Shall I not visit them for these things?*' is rhetorical.

Genuine patriotism, true nationalism, is not a product of living in an ivory tower (**9²**, cf. Ps 55⁶⁻⁸); it involves suffering with one's people and for them. See Dietrich Bonhoeffer's *Letters and Papers from Prison* (Fontana). No servant of the One who bears the sin of the world can ever look on in a detached way at those who are perishing because they do not '*know*' the Lord.

Jeremiah has noticed the way in which sins of the tongue become epidemic in a community which ignores God (**9³⁻⁸**). They are the symptoms of the poisoning of relationships which takes place whenever salvation is thought of only in material terms so that men refuse to turn to God to receive a new heart (cf. **8²⁰**).

9¹²⁻¹⁶, ²³⁻⁴: Man's true glory

True wisdom arises from a recognition of the fact that the Lord wills that there shall be love, justice and right dealing among men. But Judah will not see this.

9¹⁴. '*Baalim*'. The Hebrew plural of baal which stands here for the many local manifestations of the great Canaanite god, the husband and fertiliser of the land, the giver of rain (cf. Hos 2 ², ⁵, ⁸, ¹³, ¹⁶).

9¹⁵. '*wormwood*', '*gall*'. Bitter poisons (cf. 8¹⁴).

E

These two sections in prose are interrupted by a poem (9^{17-22}), but can be dealt with together. A true prophet is one '*to whom the mouth of the Lord hath spoken, that he may declare it*' (verse 12); he is one who lives in that fear of the Lord which is the beginning of wisdom, because he has '*knowledge*' of God and '*understands*' Him (verse 24; cf. 23^{18}, Hos 14^9). He knows that sin means a flouting of the will of the Lord— that kind of 'self-fulfilment' which is following one's own way —and its wages is death (verses 13-16).

Jeremiah knows how readily men give honour, sometimes to the great soldier, sometimes to the rich man, even sometimes to the scholar (verse 23): but what God wills is that each man should be a saint, leading a life in which God's faithfulness is reflected, a life in which there is something of the same justice and righteousness and unfailing love as is shown by His Lord (cf. verse 24).

Three important words are used in verse 24 to describe the activity of the Lord, and the nature of the activity that He expects of His people: '*lovingkindness*', '*judgement*' and '*righteousness*'. God's *chesed* or '*lovingkindness*' (sometimes translated 'mercy' in *RV*) is His utterly trustworthy covenant-love, His unfailing loyalty to His promises (cf. commentary on 2^{1-3} and 3^6-4^2). In the NT this activity is described as His 'grace' (*charis* in Greek). It is the love that never fails (1 Cor 13^8), the love that God *is*. God's *chesed* is the '*grace and truth*' that came by Jesus Christ (cf. Jn $1^{14, 17}$). The only proper response to God's *chesed*, the response of the man who '*understandeth and knoweth*' (verse 24), is to be found where the nature of the Lord is reflected in grateful, consistent, loyal and warm devotion. This involves a new creation which brings into existence man made in the image of God. (Cf. 2^2 where *chesed*, translated '*kindness*', describes Israel's response in the days when she was faithful.) See *NHS*, pp. 94-127.

'*Judgement*' (*mishpat* in Hebrew) is translated as '*ordinance*' in 8^7 (but see *RV*m). It is the God-appointed way which has been made by continued custom: it is, as it were, the accepted way of behaviour among members of God's family, the established fashion of doing things which is in character and of a piece with the tradition of the Lord's own people. In a legal context *mishpat* stands for 'case law' as distinct from legislation. A stranger cannot be expected to know the *mishpat* of the Lord (cf. 2 Kings 17^{26}). God's good manners can only be known by following Him, by companying with Him; they are the expression of His covenant-love and therefore transcend justice as we know it. Morality is not a matter of knowing the right rules, but of knowing the right Person.

'*Righteousness*' (*tsedaqah* in Hebrew) is linked with '*judgement*' also in 4², 22³, 33¹⁵; cf. Amos 5²⁴. It is something done, something that the Lord '*exercises*'; it is His activity for the salvation of His creatures, His dependants (cf. Isa 45⁸, 51⁴⁻⁵, 62¹, 45²¹). The Lord is known to be 'righteous' because He is continually at work to bring all things into a condition that satisfies Himself. Such activity involves far more than what is usually implied by justice; it shows itself in a compassionate concern for all the needy of the earth (cf. Ps 72¹²⁻¹⁴, Lk 1⁵¹⁻⁵). Therefore the 'righteous' man is not someone who is striving to observe some lofty ethical code, but the man who is permitted and enabled by the grace of God to work together with the Lord who has shown Himself to be righteous by saving him. The righteous man is a man who has faith in his righteous Lord, and his righteousness is the fruit of that trust in his Saviour. Now that the 'righteousness' of God has been 'revealed' in the coming of His Son to save the sinners who put their trust in Him (cf. Rom 1¹⁶⁻¹⁷), it is in Jesus Christ that God offers His righteousness to us. When He dwells in us and we in Him, the righteousness that He imparts is evident in our love for God and for our neighbour. (See *NHS*, pp. 59-78, 161-73). Clearly we shall not 'arrive at' this righteousness 'by works' since it is 'a righteousness which is of faith' (Rom 9³⁰⁻³).

> *Jesu, Thy blood and righteousness*
> *My beauty are, my glorious dress* . . .   (*MHB* 370)

If we must have something to boast about (9²⁴), let it be that 'while we were yet sinners' God chose to help us to know and understand Himself, by becoming our Saviour through the exercise of His '*loving kindness, judgement and righteousness*'. For the people who can boast about this are His '*delight*'.

9¹⁷⁻²²: Daughters of Jerusalem

The professional mourners are summoned to lament for the ruin of Zion, because, in the approaching epidemic of death, corpses will be spread like manure on the fields.

9¹⁷. '*cunning*'. In the sense of 'skilled'. (For professional mourners see Ezek 32¹⁶, 2 Chr 35²⁵, Mk 5³⁸, Mt 11¹⁷.)

9²¹. '*to cut off . . . from the streets*'. Better 'to cut off the children from the streets, and the young men from the open spaces' (cf. *RSV*).

9²². '*the handful*'. This was the corn that was gathered by the reaper in his left arm while he slashed at the stalks with his reaping hook. He then let it fall behind him, leaving it for someone to '*gather*' later.

The professional mourners are to teach their daughters and neighbours their craft, so that they also will know how to lament. For death is coming so terribly upon Jerusalem that corpses will suffer the last indignity of receiving no burial and will lie instead like swaths of wheat that no one is coming to gather up. In this short poem the prophet is again trying to bring home forcibly to an apostate people the truth that the '*fruit of their thoughts*' (6¹⁹), thoughts which take no account of the Lord, can only be an ungathered harvest of corpses.

9²⁵⁻⁶: God's people are heathen

Circumcision does not protect Gentiles from the punishment of the Lord; neither will it protect Judah and Israel.

9²⁵. '*in their uncircumcision*'. Better, 'and yet "uncircumcised" ' (cf. *RSV*).

9²⁶. '*that have the corners of their hair polled*'. This seems to have been a custom practised by some tribes in honour of a wine-god (cf. 25²³, 49³², Lev 19²⁷).
　　'*uncircumcised in heart*'. With hearts that refuse to know and belong to the Lord (cf. 4⁴). The phrase is synonymous with '*in their uncircumcision*' (verse 1).

The prophet reminds his people that circumcision, which is considered so important by the men of Judah, is far from being unknown among Gentile peoples. The people of Judah may say 'but these Gentiles are uncircumcised in the real meaning of the word'. But that applies to Judah also, to '*all the house of Israel*', says Jeremiah. Circumcision can have value only if it is the sign of a changed 'heart', if it denotes a personality completely subject to the Lord. See commentary on **4⁴**. (Cf. Rom 2²⁵⁻⁹, 1 Cor 7¹⁹, Gal 5⁶, 6¹⁵.) There is always the danger that signs may become more important for us than the thing they signify.

10¹⁻²⁵: Idol scarecrows

Idols are futile: the Lord is the true and living God.

10². '*signs of heaven*'. Portents of interest to astrologers.

10⁵. '*They are like ... turned work*'. This should be, as in *RSV*, 'Their idols are like scarecrows in a cucumber field' (cf. *RV*m).

10⁷. '*doth it appertain*'. Better 'it is due'.

10⁸. '*stock*'. A chunk of wood.

10⁹. '*blue and purple*'. The expensive colours in those times.
  '*cunning men*'. Skilful craftsmen, cf. **9¹⁷**.
  '*Tarshish*'. This stands for the western limit of the known world in those times, the south of Spain.
  '*Uphaz*' has not been identified, but, as *RV*m states, some early translations from the Hebrew give 'Ophir' which was in Arabia (cf. 1 Kings 9²⁸, 10¹¹).

10¹¹. This verse is in Aramaic, not Hebrew (see *RV*m), and is almost certainly an interpolation by a later scribe.

10¹²⁻¹⁶. These verses have some similarity to the 'doxologies' which seem to intrude in places in *Amos* (cf. Amos 9⁵⁻⁶). They are repeated in **51¹⁵⁻¹⁹**.

10¹⁶. '*the former*'. Used here in the sense of 'the One who gives form to', the One who creates '*all things*'.

10¹⁷. Follow *RV*m.

10²⁰. Cf. **4²⁰**.

10²¹. '*shepherds*'. Again this stands for rulers, the leaders of the nation (cf. **3¹⁵** and comment on **2⁸**).

10²³. Cf. **15¹⁹**.

10²⁵. This passage appears to have been 'borrowed' from Psalm 79⁶⁻⁷ by some later editor of the prophecies.

Except for verses 1 and 11, this chapter is in verse. The *LXX* does not include verses 6-8 or 10 or part of verse 16, and these omissions are confirmed by one of the Dead Sea Scrolls.

The Lord is King of the Gentiles as well as of Israel (verse 7), but '*the way of the nations*' is not the '*good way*' and the Gentiles give honour to idols who are 'like scarecrows in a cucumber field' (see comment on verse 5). Idols cannot speak, walk or move; they cannot act either for good or ill. For all the wealth and skill that is lavished on them, they are useless. The Lord has formed everything that is created (verse 16). He it is who keeps the winds in store to loose them as He wills (verse 13, cf. Ps 135⁷), so that when He visits the idols they shall perish. God's '*visitation*' (verse 15) is always 'a coming for a special purpose, either to bless or to punish' (Cruden). He will also 'visit' Jerusalem to punish her, since she is giving honour to idols. She must be ready to make the most of His coming (verse 19). Her rulers must learn to accept discipline before they and the people fall into destruction. They are dull-witted and worldly because they will not recognise that men must follow Someone (verse 23) and therefore they '*have not inquired of the Lord*' (verse 21). They need to learn to pray with Jeremiah

> *Show me*, as my soul can bear,
> *The depth of inbred sin.* (*MHB* 465; cf. verse 24)

Some writers would date the whole of **10¹⁻¹⁶** not earlier than 540 BC, and many others hold that, even apart from the clear case of verses 11 and 25 (see commentary above), there is matter here that is later than Jeremiah. It is possible that the whole collection grew from a saying of Jeremiah such as that in verse 2. The instruction '*Learn not the way of the nations*' seems to be directed chiefly against astrological superstition, but what develops is an attack on idols. What-ever the origins of the chapter there is valuable material here for the preacher.

Notice the definition of fellowship implied in verse 16 (cf. Ps 73[26], Deut 32[9]). It is because God first calls and claims us that He is our '*portion*'. So also it is because Jesus calls and chooses His followers that we can say '*Our* Lord' and '*Our* Father'.

In verse 19 we are pointed to the proper antidote to the poison of self-pity, and verse 23 may move us to a deeper understanding of, and a greater gratitude for, the privilege of discipleship. We have a Lord to whom we can say 'Lead Thou me on', and

> *Teach me the happy art*
> *In all things to depend*
> *On Thee . . .   (MHB* 612, 635)

But the main theme is idolatry (cf. Isa 44[6-20], 40[12-31]). It is unlikely that Jeremiah himself ever visited Babylon (see commentary on 13[4]), but there were men in Judah who had been there as representatives of their country, humble sup-pliants on behalf of their king, and the city with its massive walls, its canals, its hanging gardens, its ziggurat (the 'Tower of Babel'), its expensive temples to Marduk, Adad and Ishtar, must have made something like the impression that is made nowadays on a young student from Africa when he visits the cities of the U.S.A. or the U.S.S.R. and sees something at first hand of their impressive technical achievements. It must have seemed to many of those who went to Babylon on behalf of the king of Judah, and to many of those who were deported there, that here in Babylon at any rate there were gods who were capable of *doing* something effective, while Yahweh, the god of Judah, can only stand by, helpless. Jeremiah will have none of that; he knows that the Lord is watchful (1[12]). It is the idols that are helpless; costly and impressive as they may be, they are still nothing but '*the work of cunning men*' (verse 9). They are really pitiful signs of the constant tendency of human beings to trust in the things that they can do and make to provide security and salvation. But there is only one Saviour, the one God who alone is worthy of trust (cf. Acts 4[12]).

Wherefore my hope is in the Lord,
My works I count but dust . . .
His helping mercy hath no bounds,
His love surpasseth all. (*MHB* 359)

Mr. Fred Hoyle pointed out that 'it can hardly be denied that the cosmology of the ancient Hebrews is only the merest daub compared with the sweeping grandeur of the picture revealed by modern science' (*The Nature of the Universe*, p. 115). He goes on to assert 'that religion is but a blind attempt to find an escape from the truly dreadful situation in which we find ourselves'. He does not seem to realize that the prophets would have agreed with him in this; they knew that 'religion' is a man-made thing and very different from a firm trust in the *'former of all things'* and from loyal, grateful obedience to the only Saviour, the *'King of the nations'* (10[7, 16]).

John Calvin described the heart of man as an 'idol-factory'. No preacher should regard idolatry as an out-of-date subject. We have always to be on our guard against substituting an 'image' for the living God, against worshipping our own home-made idea of God, against serving some god whom we can persuade to do what *we* want, some 'idol' that allows us to forget that we are required to do what God wants. This is a more subtle form of idolatry than the tendency to substitute other things for God as the goal of our efforts—nation, church, political party, power, progress, justice, truth, duty, brother-hood, world peace—almost anything can be made to serve in place of the *'true'* and *'living'* God (cf. verse 10).

Notice also that we are not to encourage our leaders when they follow *'the way of the nations'*, when they accept the standards and ideals of this world instead of seeking the counsel of the Lord (verse 21; cf. 1 Sam 8[4-9]). They need the prayers of the Church and the active help of Christian citizens, that they may be saved from the temptation to be great in their own fashion, from trust in the powers of this world or in the gods of the 'great' powers, and from thinking that in the 'practical business of statecraft', the Lordship of God is irrelevant.

11[1-17]: God's covenant-love is refused

Jeremiah must recall God's people to the covenant He gave to them in Moses' day, because the Bride of the Lord has clearly no right to be in His house if she will not be faithful to Him.

11⁴. '*iron furnace*'. A furnace for smelting iron (a metaphor for severe trials, cf. Deut 4²⁰, 1 Kings 8⁵¹).

11⁹. '*conspiracy*'. Better 'breach of faith', or 'revolt' (*RSV*).

11¹². '*incense*'. Better 'sacrifice'. So also in verses 13 and 17.

11¹⁵. '*seeing she hath wrought . . . thou rejoicest*'. The *RV*m states that 'the text is obscure', but this is one of the places in *Jeremiah* where the *LXX* may have preserved the correct reading. With its help we get something like 'seeing that she has acted wickedly. Can solemn promises or sacrificial meat avert thy fate, or canst thou escape by them?' (Cf. the *RSV* which also appears to be based on the *LXX*.) The point that is being made is apparently similar to 7²¹⁻³.

Many scholars have maintained that this passage indicates that Jeremiah supported the 'reformation' in the days of Josiah. But it seems better to regard the passage as a summary in prose of much of the prophet's teaching, followed by a brief poem (verses 15-16) of which the Hebrew text is badly preserved. The people are to be reminded of the relationship which God established between them and Himself when He delivered them from Egypt and gave them the Covenant (verse 4; cf. Ex. 24). For nearly a thousand years He has continued to approach them with His living word, and has used many methods of encouraging them to remember and obey Him, but they refuse to be His people (verses 7-8). They have gone further and further from Him and are incorrigible, past praying for (verse 14, cf 7¹⁶, 14¹¹). What was once the Israel of God, the Lord's fair 'olive tree' (verse 16; cf. Ps 52⁸, Hos 14⁶), has no longer any right to be in His Temple and must be blasted by lightning. Sacrifices of meat and fat are of no use in such a situation.

Here we have in another form the prophet's insistence on the need for a *new* heart and a *new* covenant (cf. 31³¹⁻⁴). This is the only hope for people who, although they have been given God's covenant simply because He had 'a favour unto them' (Ps 44³), nevertheless are persisting in walking '*in the stubbornness of their evil heart*' (verse 8). The gospel is that such a new covenant has now been given, and that such a new heart can now be received, because God has 'a favour unto' us.

11¹⁸⁻²³: The men of Anathoth

Jeremiah was like an innocent lamb on the way to the slaughter, until the Lord warned him that he was in danger. The people of Anathoth, who have threatened him with death unless he gives up prophesying, will themselves be punished by God.

11¹⁸. This is the beginning of a new section, different from verses 1-17. Read 'And the Lord gave me knowledge, and I knew'.

11¹⁹. '*let us cut him off* . . . '. Since the prophet was unmarried (16²), there could be no descendants to carry on '*his name*'.

11²⁰. '*that triest the reins and heart*'. The '*reins*' or 'kidneys' were regarded as the seat of strong emotion (cf. commentary on 4¹⁹). The meaning is that God knows what is in men, even their most secret feelings and motives (cf. **17²⁰, 20¹²**).

11²³. '*there shall be no remnant*'. What they threatened to do to Jeremiah (see commentary on verse 19) will in fact happen to them. The punishment will fit the crime; we are told in **12³** that it is the men of Anathoth who are to be '*like sheep for the slaughter*'.

There have been many conjectures about the reason for this plot, and about the date of the incident. The reason may simply have been that the madman from Anathoth (cf. **29²⁶**) was getting his family and his home town a bad name. If the incident came early in the career of the prophet, God may have used it to say to him 'Leave Anathoth and go to Jerusalem'. Verse 19 has probably influenced Isaiah 53⁷⁻⁸ (although a different Hebrew word for '*lamb*' is used there), and there are scholars who believe that Jeremiah himself was one of the sources of the poet's concept of the 'Servant of the Lord'.

There was nothing that Jeremiah would have liked more

than to be at peace with all men, yet his calling led him into situations where every man's hand seemed to be against him (cf. **15¹⁰**). Even his own family and townspeople are against him; his enemies are 'the men of his own house' (Mic 7⁶). Every man was expected to work with the others for the good of his family and clan, but these people in Anathoth are plotting against one of their own number. There could be no plainer illustration of the fact that society in Judah is collapsing into chaos, and that men have forfeited the 'peace' that can exist only when God's people accept their proper covenant-relationship with their Lord. The intention of the conspirators is to destroy the prophecies by doing away with the prophesier. But their name, not his, is the one that will be rooted out (verse 23). It is the shock of discovering that kinsfolk (cf. **12⁶**) can behave like this which stings Jeremiah into crying for vengeance, into appealing for the Lord's judgement (verse 20).

When Jesus came to His own people, they did not welcome Him; His townsfolk had little use for Him, His friends thought that He was mad, and His family tried to restrain Him (see Jn 1¹¹, Mk 3²¹, ³¹, Lk 4²⁸⁻⁹). Jeremiah was not able to pray 'forgive them, for they know not what they do'. Jesus 'when he was reviled, reviled not again; when he suffered threatened not; but committed himself to him that judgeth righteously' (1 Pet 2²³). It is from Him that we learn that we are to love our enemies. Apart from His grace, we shall do no better, and probably worse, than Jeremiah. He knew nothing of the Risen Saviour who offers men a share in His eternal life, so that he could only expect the Lord to vindicate him *on earth*.

Other suggestions for the preacher will be found towards the close of the commentary on the next section.

12¹⁻¹³: Why do the wicked prosper?

When the prophet complains that the wicked are allowed to flourish in security, he is told that he will have to face even more difficult problems than this—the treachery of his own kinsmen, and the sight of the Lord delivering up His people into the hand of their enemies.

12¹. Jeremiah has a case to plead (cf. *RV*m).

12². '*reins*'. See commentary on **11²⁰**.

12³. '*prepare them*'. See *RV*m. They are to be 'set apart'.

12⁴. '*herbs*'. Better 'grass'.

'*our latter end*'. They think that God takes no notice of what they do—another description of people who are atheist in their behaviour, however devout they may appear to be in public worship.

12⁵. *RSV* is helpful here. If the prophet is stumbling in easy country, what is he going to do in the swampy jungle? ('*the pride of Jordan*' is the thickly overgrown tropical swamp along the edge of the river).

12⁹. '*speckled bird*'. This may be the francolin or black partridge, a handsome game-bird, speckled like a guinea-fowl, which is an easy catch for falcons and other birds of prey. See the *Preacher's Quarterly*, June 1956, pp. 162f. Whether this is correct or not, the point seems to be that the other birds attack this one because it looks different from themselves.

12¹⁰. '*shepherds*'. See commentary on **2⁸**. The rulers of Judah have destroyed the Lord's '*vineyard*', which is the people He has entrusted to them.

12¹¹. '*it mourneth unto me*'. Read 'to my sorrow' and cf. **31²⁰**.

12¹³. '*ye shall be ashamed*'. Read 'they shall be ashamed', (cf. *RV*m).

For the first time in the Old Testament, the question is asked, 'Why are bad people allowed to keep on getting away with it?' (cf. Hab 1⁵⁻¹³, Ps 73, Job 21⁷). But the prophet is not raising it as a mere abstract problem: it is a question that has to be asked by a man of faith, and he has to put it *to God*. Jeremiah receives no direct answer to his question. Instead the Lord warns him that his worst troubles are still to come. If he is falling down in safe territory, what is going to happen when he comes to the jungle (verse 5)? The '*pride of Jordan*' could be seen from Anathoth; it was not only very difficult going, but it was also the haunt of wild animals (cf. **49¹⁹**). The prophet is being led out of a life of conventional 'security' into a jungle where every man's hand is against him. But this is only to be expected since he serves God. Just as God's foes are His own people, so the prophet's foes will be his own people (verses 7-8). It is not only Jeremiah who suffers: God also has had to abandon His house and give up the family that has turned on Him. God has had to abandon His people to wrath; they have driven Him away and are bringing destruction upon themselves (verse 13). It is hardly surprising that this pattern is reflected in the experience of His prophet.

In these verses we have one of a number of indications that the prophet's own suffering acted as a gateway to a recognition and a dim understanding of the suffering of God (cf. **45**[4-5]). Like Jeremiah long ago, preachers are people who have to learn things as well as to teach things (verse 5). Problems that can be dealt with confidently, so long as we can treat them as more or less abstract theological problems, may have to become personal to ourselves before they are really appreciated. Though we try, and indeed we must, to find the reason for puzzling aspects of life, we shall sometimes meet situations for which there is no really satisfactory intellectual solution. But we can also recognize how blessed is the man who has learned to walk with the Lord in the valley of deep shadows, where we can be supported because we find that we are not alone but are truly sharing in His sorrow (verse 11). Men can be destroyed, not because they are abandoned, but because they themselves abandon God (verse 12). Here is a continuing impulse to evangelism:

> *For those that will not come to Him*
> *The ransom of His life was paid.* (*MHB* 75)

The Lord knows all our motives; He tests '*the reins and the heart*' (verse 2, cf. **11**[20]). Our motives for questioning Him and even our motives for warning the wicked are open to Him. Christ needs no one to tell Him what is in us (cf. Rev 2[23], Jn 2[25], 4[39]).

> *Thou judgest us: Thy purity*
> *Doth all our lusts condemn . . .*
> *Our thoughts lie open to Thy sight;*
> *And naked to Thy glance . . .* (*MHB* 103)

He knows how readily we may take the name of God on our lips, how our hypocrisy spoils God's creation (cf. verse 4 and 12$^{10-13}$). Yet He still chooses us, and allows us to share in His work (cf. Jn 15$^{18-21}$, 2 Cor 4$^{10-11}$, Phil 1^{29}).

12$^{14-17}$: The Hope of Israel

Judah shall be restored and her foes punished, though any Gentile nation that obeys the Lord will prosper also.

This word seems to come from a later period than the rest of the chapter. It asserts (cf. 1^{10}) that the Lord of the nations is able to discipline and restore the Gentiles, even as He disciplines and restores Judah. Since it appears that some people from Judah are already in exile (verse 14), the saying may date from the time of Zedekiah, or even later. God's purpose is always to have mercy; if only men would '*diligently learn the ways of my people*' (verse 16) instead of '*the way of the nations*' (10^2), it would be possible to fulfil the promise of building and planting, as well as the promise of the breaking down and overthrow of evil (cf. 16$^{19-21}$).

This is a possible starting point for preaching about the 'missionary message of the Old Testament' (cf. Isa 56$^{6-8}$, 49^6). Israel is of one blood with the nations of the earth (Gen 5^{10}), and her very existence is to serve as a witness before all the nations to the God who can save, and who wills to save, all men. This seed in the OT burst into flower on the day of Pentecost, and from then on the Holy Spirit is sending representatives of God's people into all the world to teach '*the ways of my people*', in the sure faith that Jesus is the Way, the Truth and the Life.

The creation still awaits the time when the children of Abraham after the flesh will see that their suffering can be united with the suffering of the Son of God in the working out of His purposes for the universe. God had a people long before the gospel came to Gentiles such as ourselves, who have been grafted 'against all nature . . . into the cultivated olive' (Rom 11^{24} in *NEB*), and therefore the Church is set in a special relationship with the Jews, not only the ancient Jews but also the Jews who live alongside us today. Without them we cannot be made perfect,—nor they without us.

13^{1–11}: The sign of the loincloth

The prophet is instructed to wear a new loincloth and then to bury it near the river for some time. When he digs it up again it is useless. Even so Judah has become useless, since she has ceased to cling to the Lord.

13¹. '*girdle*'. The cloth is not a girdle, which was worn over other garments, but a 'loincloth' worn next to the skin.

'*linen*'. This was worn by priests (Lev 16⁴), and may be prescribed here as a reminder to God's people that they are holy to Him.

13⁴. '*Euphrates*'. Even though '*rock*' may suggest the upper reaches near Carchemish, two journeys to the Euphrates and back must have taken a very long time. It has been suggested that some other stream was made to represent the Euphrates. Because of a similarity in name in the Hebrew, it is suggested that the cloth was in fact buried in the Wadi Parah, which is only three miles from Anathoth. But this linking of Parah with 'Perath' ('*Euphrates*') is not very convincing. The difficulty would disappear if this were the description of a vision, rather than two actual journeys to and fro, but nothing is said in the text about a vision, and the difficulty remains.

Fortunately, the meaning of this acted parable seems reasonably clear. God's people, who are meant to cling to Him and Him alone, have turned aside and therefore have become '*profitable for nothing*' (verse 10). They '*refuse to hear*' His word, they '*walk in the stubbornness of their heart*' and this leads to going '*after other gods, to serve them, and to worship them*' (verse 10). So the people that were meant to be holy to the Lord are ruined, and have become useless to Him. By turning to the gods of Mesopotamia and attempting to give them a place alongside the Lord, they have in fact ceased to cleave to the living God, and they can no longer be unto Him '*for a people, and for a name, and for a praise, and for a glory*' (verse 11). This message may come from the time when Jehoiakim transferred his allegiance from Egypt to Babylon, soon after the Chaldeans had driven the Egyptians back from Carchemish into their own country.

God has bound His people to Himself. He is with them always, and He will not suffer His holy one to see corruption (Acts 2²⁷, Ps 16¹⁰), whereas those who leave Him can only rot like linen in the damp earth. So it is with any man or any church that turns away from the Word of God and from the new covenant in His blood; to cease to cling to Him is the sure way to become like salt that has lost its savour and is fit 'for nothing, but to be cast out and trodden under foot of men' (Mt 5¹³).

13¹²⁻¹⁷: An awful intoxication

The Lord is about to destroy the people of Judah by dashing them against each other.

13¹². '*bottle*'. An earthenware wine-jar which would hold several gallons (cf. *RV*m).

13¹⁶. '*dark mountains*'. Better 'darkening', in the rapidly failing light of a sub-tropical nightfall (cf. *RV*m).

This comparison of the wrath of the Lord to a terrible drunkenness is used by several prophets (cf. 25¹⁵⁻²⁹, Ezek 23³²⁻⁴, Isa 51¹⁷⁻²³). But here the starting point may be a popular saying which ran, 'Every wine-jar shall be filled with wine' (cf. verse 12), which meant something like 'We've never had it so good'. The prophet insists that self-indulgence is pagan, and must lead to receiving the cup of the Lord, not in blessing (cf. Ps 23⁵, 116¹³), but in wrath. When pride withstands God, it goes before a fall (verses 15, 17), and the haughtiness that refuses to give Him His rightful place must be replaced by a proper obedience. It is only by such obedience that they can '*give glory to the Lord*' (verse 16). Their conversion from pride to obedience is urgently required since the night is falling swiftly, the '*gross darkness*' in which '*the Lord's flock is taken captive*' (verses 16-17).

Although the Lord Jesus has drunk the cup for us (Mk 14³⁶), and although He now offers us another cup in which there is life instead of the destruction we deserve (Lk 22²⁰), the preacher and the Church still have to grieve (verse 17) for the pride which makes men deaf and blind to the Word of God. The time is short, 'now is the day of salvation', and men must be called into God's marvellous light before He brings darkness upon all that has rejected Him (cf. Rev 14⁹⁻¹²).

13¹⁸⁻²⁷: How can Judah change?

Jehoiachin and Nehushta, the queen-mother, are warned of approaching disaster: since Judah has fallen into unbreakable habits of evil, the Lord will put her to shame.

13¹⁸. '*for your headtires . . . glory*'. The Hebrew is obscure (cf. *RV*m). We should probably read, with the help of the *LXX*, 'for there shall come down from your head your beautiful diadem'.

13¹⁹. '*shut up*'. Besieged; '*open*' means 'raise' the siege.

13²¹. Read 'What wilt thou say when he sets over thee as chief those whom thou hast thyself taught to be thy friends' (cf. *RV*m and *RSV*).

13²². '*thy skirts . . . thy heels*'. Probably a euphemism for rape and shameful treatment (cf. verse 26).

13²⁷. Refers to heathen rites and to the moral depravity which results from them (cf. 5⁸).

The poem in verses 18-19 refers to the 'hundred days' of the reign of Jehoiachin (Jeconiah) and the events described in 2 Kings 24⁸⁻¹⁷. The queen-mother, Nehushta, was even more important at this stage than such figures usually were because her son was still only eighteen years old. Jehoiachin inherited the trouble that the rebellion of Jehoiakim brought on Judah. The cities of southern Judah are now besieged and cannot be relieved. There is no way of turning Nebuchadrezzar back, and the '*flock*' that the young king has just started to shepherd must surely suffer (verses 19-20). It is because the Bride of the Lord has forgotten Him that she has fallen a slave to the habit of doing evil and has sought security by relying on vain things; now He delivers her up to shameful violence (verses 22, 23, 26; cf. 5⁸⁻⁹, 4³⁰). When Zedekiah is put on the throne by Nebuchadrezzar in place of Jehoiachin, the prophet warns Judah that there may be even worse trouble ahead if she still refuses to repent (verse 27).

F

Here we see how Jeremiah's close walk with God gives him insight into the power of sin. Just as a nation that ignores God may find that its former allies have now become its masters (verse 21), so individuals who are '*accustomed to do evil*' are liable to find that they have become its hopeless slaves, and that they have lost even the will to be clean again (verses 23, 27). It is interesting to compare the *RSV* of the second half of verse 27 with the *RV*. The *RSV* translation is more accurate, but there is truth in the *RV* phrase '*thou wilt not be made clean*'. God's will is that His people shall be clean, but they themselves may lose the will to be clean if they forget Him and trust in falsehoods (verse 25). It is as impossible for any of us to make ourselves clean by our own efforts as it is for the leopard to change his spots (verse 23). But the gospel is that the longing of God that we shall be clean can be fulfilled (cf. verse 27 in *RSV*).

> *Though earth and hell the word gainsay,*
>   *The word of God can never fail;*
> *The Lamb shall take my sins away,*
>   *'Tis certain, though impossible . . .*   (*MHB* 548)

This is the answer to the pessimism one encounters in those who say, 'Well, it's only human nature, and you can't do anything about that'. God *wills* to make us clean: His love, whether manifested in blessing or in discipline, has that very purpose. Christ is able to break the 'power of cancelled sin' and 'set the prisoner free' (*MHB* 1). But, for those who will not have Him to be their Saviour, for those who reject all the drawing power of the Man lifted up from the earth, there can be but one end; for those who choose '*the portion measured unto*' them from the Lord (verse 25), the end is terrible beyond all imagining (cf. Jn 8 21-3, 31-47, Mk 3 28-30).

14 1-10: Drought

A great drought leads people to pray that the Lord will be with His people. But He cannot remain with those who delight to go on doing evil.

14 1. This is an editorial heading to the section.

14 3. '*pits*'. These are underground cisterns. Because they are empty, those who depend on them for their water supply '*cover their heads*' with grief.

14⁵. '*hind*'. This animal was a proverb for its devotion to its young, and the '*wild asses*' for their hardiness.

14⁹. '*astonied*'. Confused, bewildered.

14¹⁰. Cf. Hosea 8¹³.

Even in this terrible drought, which affects townsfolk, farmers and wild animals alike, the people are blaming the Lord instead of themselves (verses 8-9). Therefore, even when they 'confess their sin' and invoke God's mercy, His answer to their prayer must be, 'No'.

When things appear to be going well it may seem to be enough to pay only occasional, fleeting visits to God; when real trouble comes, however, we are inclined to think that He is to blame for paying only occasional, fleeting visits to us (verse 8). It is when trouble comes that we are most ready to remember that '*we are called by*' His '*name*', although the relationship may have meant little or nothing to us before (verse 10). It may sometimes seem that God is an aloof spectator of our troubles, but that may be because, in our case too, there have been occasions when He 'came to his own home, and his own people received him not' (*RSV* of Jn 1¹¹). The coming of Jesus is the sign that God is not a remote President of the Immortals who enjoys His sport, but that He wills to be God-with-us at all times, to *abide* with His people for their good. To all those who receive Him He gives power to 'become children of God' (Jn 1¹³), and the blessedness of discovering that, if they suffer, they suffer *with Him*.

14¹¹⁻¹⁶: False prophets

The Lord instructs Jeremiah not to pray for his people, and again reminds him that the false prophets will come to a terrible end.

14¹⁴. '*and divination, and a thing of nought*'. This should read 'and divination which is useless'; cf. *RSV*.

This paragraph is in prose, whereas the rest of chapter **14** is in verse. The people of Judah are past praying for (verse 11; cf. **7¹⁶, 11¹⁴**), but the prophet points out that they are being misled by false prophets, men who claim to speak for God and yet proclaim peace where there is no peace (verse 13; cf. **6¹³⁻¹⁴, 23⁹⁻³³, 28¹⁻¹⁷**). The test of a true prophet is his relationship to the Lord; everything depends on whether God '*sent*' him, whether God '*commanded*' him, whether God '*spake*' to him (verse 14). Unless there is a continuing relationship with God, all that a man can produce is the '*deceit*' of his '*own heart*'; no matter how well-intentioned he may be, he can only mislead those to whom he prophesies. Those who lap up such '*deceit*' are not without their own responsibility and they will have to drink a bitter cup when their own '*wickedness*' is poured '*upon them*' (verse 16).

Preachers must beware of peddling their own dreams and brainwaves (**23⁸**), their home-made comfortable words, as if these were from the Lord. If they do, it will be the blind leading the blind, and an evil day is in store for them (verse 15). Congregations too are not without their own responsibility: they must not expect and encourage such preaching. They must not seek any 'peace' other than that which keeps guard over the 'hearts' and 'thoughts' of those who are 'in Christ Jesus' (Phil 4⁷).

14¹⁷-15⁴: Confession

Judah confesses her sin and pleads with the Lord not to cancel His covenant. But plague, war, famine and exile are coming.

14¹⁸. '*go about*'. Better 'trade' (cf. *RV*m). They are hucksters with misleading messages.

15¹. '*stood*'. The attitude of prayer.

15². '*death*'. Better 'plague'.

15³. '*dogs*'. Not lapdogs but scavengers.

15⁴. '*because of Manasseh* . . .'. This is possibly a kind of

editorial footnote, or even perhaps the editors' heading for
the next section.

God's people have their prophets and their priests, but these
leaders are without the thing that is essential: they have no
'*knowledge*'. No matter what claims they may make, it is
clear from their way of life that they do not '*know*' the Lord.
Among all the trouble that Judah is suffering, and in face of
the even worse trouble that is looming up, these people go
on with their business as usual, peddling what they claim is
the word of the Lord. They are like roaming madmen (14¹⁸).
So it comes about that, even though the drought continues,
God's people continue to be incapable of genuine repentance.
They are still trusting in a Temple which they misuse, and in
the Covenant which they have not kept (14²¹⁻²). Even though
Moses and Samuel, those two mighty intercessors, were to
pray for them, God's answer to their plea would still have
to be, 'No' (15¹). (It should perhaps be noticed that the
intercessions of Moses and Samuel had been on behalf of
repentant people; cf. Ex 32¹¹⁻¹⁴, ³², 1 Sam 7⁹.) Since the
people of Judah persist in acting like heathens, God will
make them 'a horror to all the kingdoms of the earth' (*RSV*
of 15⁴). Jeremiah is not free to promise his people anything
better than destruction; the Lord's answer to the question,
'Hast thou utterly rejected Judah?' (14¹⁹) is 'Yes'.

Preachers are not called to be tipsters with a stock of
counterfeit 'words of God' (14¹⁸). Their constant care should
be to serve the Word of God, the One who says, 'Follow Me'.
The true wellbeing of the people of God depends on keeping
the pulpit free of the fancies of our own minds, and on allowing
nothing but 'the love of Christ' to 'constrain' us. Only then
is there hope that the Church may be the 'throne of God's
glory', and the place where His covenant is kept. This is why
the faithful preacher is given the guidance of the Holy Spirit.

15⁵⁻⁹: Distress

The Lord can hold His hand no longer: Judah must fall.

15⁶. '*weary with repenting*'. That is 'tired of relenting'.

15⁷. '*I have fanned them with a fan*'. Better 'I have winnowed thee with a winnowing fork', as in *RSV* (cf. Mt 3¹², Ps 1⁴).

15⁸. Follow *RV*m.

15⁹. '*given up the ghost*'. Better 'swooned'.

Because Judah has rejected Him (verse 6), God's 'ceaseless, unexhausted love', which always 'delights our evil to remove' (*MHB* 49), must in this case take the form of judgement. It will be widows who will be more numerous than 'the sand of the seas', not the descendants of Abraham (cf. Gen 22¹⁷, etc.). The mother of '*seven*' who in normal times would be regarded as the most fortunate woman in all Judah, will lose all that she treasures with the death of her children. Even those people who escape the other terrors that are coming will be certain to fall to the sword (verses 8-9, cf. 1 Sam 2⁵, Ruth 4¹⁵).

We are to take care that we do not let 'the grace of God' which we have received 'go for nothing' (2 Cor 6¹ in *NEB*); even in those times when it seems that it is 'yet day', and all is bright for us, we need to be kept in mind that the night is surely coming for those who persistently refuse to repent.

15¹⁰⁻²¹: 'Alone, alone, all, all alone'

Jeremiah is sorry that he was ever born; he cannot bear it that he must continually be stirring up opposition and be encountering ridicule and reproach for the Lord's sake. He constantly intercedes for his people, yet he meets with their persistent and adamant opposition. His calling has led to his being isolated from his fellow men, and now he fears that the Lord also may desert him. But the Lord's reply is that His prophet must himself be cleansed of all impurity so that, with His Lord's aid, he may become really strong to prevail against the continuing opposition of the wicked.

15¹⁰. '*earth*'. This should be 'land'; he is a prophet to the nations, but it is in Judah that he meets with opposition.
'*on usury*'. These words should be omitted (cf. *RSV*); the

point is that he has been 'neither a borrower nor a lender' (*Hamlet*, Act I, Scene 3).

15¹¹. The Hebrew is difficult (see *RV*m). Read, 'Let it be so, Lord, if I have not pleaded with thee for good; if I have not interceded with thee for the enemy, in time of evil and time of affliction' (cf. **17¹⁶, 18²⁰**).

15¹². Again the Hebrew is difficult. Follow *RV*m.

15¹³⁻¹⁴. These verses recur in **17³⁻⁴** where the context is more appropriate.

15¹⁵. '*Take me not away in thy long suffering*'. He hopes that the Lord's patience with those who are persecuting His prophet will not mean that His vengeance falls upon them only after he is dead and gone. The prophet wants to be alive to see it.

15¹⁶. '*I am called by thy name*'. He is the Lord's special possession and therefore deserves, and can expect, His special protection.

15¹⁸. '*waters that fail*'. See *RV*m. He fears that even the Lord may fail him when he is most in need of help, like a stream that gives promise of a good water supply and then fails and peters out when it is most needed.

Jeremiah is now finding in his own nature something of the very fault that has ruined Judah—the tendency to shake free from the ties of God's love, the attempt to set a limit beyond which faith in Him will not go. This refusal to trust God beyond a certain point is in fact a forsaking of Him, and is the root of every kind of evil. Of course Jeremiah has gone much farther than most men; he has constantly prayed for the welfare of those who despitefully use him, and he has battled resolutely for their welfare in spite of all their stubbornness. But 'there are limits!'; he cannot bear to be unpopular all the time, he cannot stand being put in Coventry, and there is always the nagging fear that some day even the last link will snap and the Lord Himself will not stand by Him. The prophet could so easily have been 'modest' and retired quietly; after all, who was he to maintain that he was the only man in the whole battalion who was in step? Who was he to go in face of public opinion and claim that it was the other prophets who were 'false'? What clearer proof can there be that a man is mentally unbalanced when he will not accept the opinion of the experts and the experienced leaders that he is wrong? After all, the Lord seems to be in no hurry to deal with Jeremiah's opponents—He gives no sign that they are opposing Him by attacking the man from Anathoth. . . .

Surely no man had more right to expect sympathy and comfort from his Master—but the Lord's reply is stern: His prophet needs to be converted and to grow in holiness. The prophet must repent. Only then may the Lord fulfil the promises that He made when He brought him into His service (cf. 1¹⁷⁻¹⁹). He is a prophet only because he belongs to his Lord, only because he is '*called by*' the '*name*' of Him whose words are '*found*' by His appointed spokesmen. Jeremiah's doubt that the Fountain of living water (2¹³) may be '*deceitful*' (verse 18) is an indication that he still needs to have the precious separated from the base metal in himself (verse 19, cf. commentary on 6²⁷⁻³⁰). The only way out of his trouble is to go deeper into it, and through it, in faith. Only then can he be as God's '*mouth*' (verse 19); only then will his life confirm his message, for he will have discovered in his own experience the Lord's power to '*deliver*' and '*redeem*' (verse 21; cf. Ex 4¹⁶). Jeremiah has often been described as a great individual, standing out from the mass of the people, but clearly he is whatever he is only because of the activity of God. (The '*hand*' of God (verse 17) is God Himself at work, shaping the personality of His prophet. Cf. 1⁹, Isa 8¹¹, Ezek 1³, 37¹.)

Faith is like a rope that sometimes frays until only one frail-looking thread holds—the thread that still leads a man to complain *to God*. Jeremiah would have agreed with Theodor Haeker when he writes in his *Journal in the Night*, 'Never leave hold of God! Love Him! And if for the moment you cannot love Him, then fight with Him, accuse Him, argue with Him like Job,'—or Jeremiah—'and if you can, slander Him, blaspheme Him—but never leave Him! For then you will become very ridiculous and wretched and—worst of all, you will not even notice it.' (I owe the quotation to Alec Robertson's autobiography, *More than Music*.)

We all hate to be classed as 'different'. There are people who are even more afraid of being *thought* a prig than they are of *being* a prig. No one, least of all young people, likes to be the odd man out—the only one in the office who doesn't go in for the football pool or sweepstake, the only one in the trade union branch who votes against a resolution, the only one in the coach-party who doesn't drink beer, and so on. Of course, there are also people who take pleasure in being different occasionally, who disregard convention for the mere sake of being different. Jeremiah would have disagreed with both these attitudes. He knew in his very bones that man is made for community; to be a human being is to be a creature that needs fellowship. But what is even more important is that it is *God* who has made us like this and we cannot have genuine fellowship until our relationship with God is right.

'Peace among men' is the will of God, but He may have to take away His peace from us (cf. **16⁵**) to teach us that we are to seek first His kingdom and His righteousness. We are not to set easy relationships with other people before our loyalty to God, any more than we are to throw our weight about because we 'dearly love a good scrap'. We can only have a right relationship with other people *through* Jesus Christ our Lord. When we find ourselves unpopular or 'sent to Coventry', we shall be tempted to rebel and, like Jeremiah, we shall probably need to repent and obey the Lord's command to '*take forth the precious from the vile*' (verse 19). Unlike the prophet we shall be able to turn to the example of the perfect submission of Jesus (cf. Mk 14³⁶), and have the consolation of knowing that, if we suffer for the sake of God's eternal purpose to bring all men into a fellowship of reconciliation through His Son, we suffer in fellowship with the whole Church.

'*I did eat them*', in verse 16, is an idea that is developed later, (in Ezek 2⁸-3³, Rev 10⁹⁻¹⁰), although there is no suggestion here that the '*words*' were in written form on a scroll. (Cf. also Jn 4³²⁻³⁴, Job 23¹², Ps 119¹⁰³, Mt 4⁴.) The prophet finds that the word which is sometimes '*a joy*' can also be painful; it can inflict a wound, like that of Amfortas in the legend of the Grail, which refuses '*to be healed*' (verse 18). But it will be healed by the One whose 'dazzling body' still bears the 'tokens of His passion' (*MHB* 264).

16¹⁻²¹: The cost of discipleship

As a sign that parents will soon be mourning the death of their children throughout Judah, the prophet is forbidden to marry and have children. As a sign that it will soon be impossible for anyone to carry out conventional mourning customs, he is forbidden to share in mourning now. As a sign that all rejoicing will soon become impossible, he is forbidden to share in feasts. For the people have forsaken the Lord and are worshipping other gods. Such punishment is about to fall upon them that they, and the Gentiles also, will know beyond all doubt that the Lord is God.

16¹. '*to me*'. Notice that this chapter is in the first person, a piece of autobiography.

16⁶⁻⁷. '*cut*', '*make themselves bald*', etc. These were mourning customs. The 'bread' (notice *RV*m) and the '*cup of consolation*' were brought to the mourners by neighbours and friends.

16¹³. There is a play here on the name 'Jeremiah', which means 'God hurls': 'I will hurl you out of this land' (*RSV*).

16¹⁴⁻¹⁵. These verses recur in 23⁷⁻⁸ where they seem to be more appropriately placed.

16¹⁸. '*double*'. This indicates heavy punishment, not twice as much as is deserved (cf. Isa 40²).

16¹⁹⁻²⁰. These verses are in verse, but the rest of the chapter is prose.

Here we have some indication of what is described (in the title of one of Dietrich Bonhoeffer's books) as *The Cost of Discipleship*. It is by his life as well as his doctrine, that Jeremiah has to tell his people that they are rushing heedlessly away from God into terrible disaster. His loneliness (cf. 15¹⁷) extends even to his not being free to marry and have a family (verse 2, cf. 1 Cor 7²⁶). It was most unusual for any Hebrew to be celibate and that makes this 'sign' the more striking. God had used the married life of other prophets to illustrate His word (cf. Hos 2$^{1-9}$; Isa 8$^{3-4}$; Ezek 24$^{15-27}$), but in this case it is a prophet's celibacy that is required.

As a further indication of the evil things that are coming upon a people that has forsaken its Lord (verses 11, 16), Jeremiah is not permitted to rejoice with them that rejoice or to weep with them that weep (verses 5, 8). This is what is involved in being 'known' by God (cf. 1^5); his whole life is to be filled 'in every part' with witness. In even the most common things of everyday behaviour he has to proclaim to men who *'hearken not unto'* the Lord (verse 12) that punishment must come. If they will attend to idols, lifeless images which pollute the land like *'carcases'* (verse 18) they will bring about a state of affairs in which normal life becomes impossible for anyone. But all God's dealing with His people has a missionary purpose, and the days are coming when all the nations will acknowledge that He is the only Lord.

Whatever led the editors to include the poem in verses 19-20 at this point, there is a reminder here that God is consistent in all that He does. Even His discipline, however terrible it may have to be, is a part of His purpose to reconcile the world to Himself, so that all men know His 'peace', His 'steadfast love and mercy' (cf. verse 5 in *RSV*). When we are deprived of that peace and love and mercy, it is because we have turned every one to his own way (cf. verse 12) and so have polluted God's creation (cf. verse 18). There is a Love that will not let us go; we cannot escape the Hound of Heaven (verse 17). We are to live by His word since we are called to be children of the living God. Any other way of life is a way of *'lies, even vanity and things wherein there is no profit'* (verse 19). Many of the things to which we give our loyalty and trust are *'gods, which yet are no gods'* (verse 20). That is why our civilised world is more full of man-made deities than any African village. That is what happens unless men are living out God's word in every part of their lives.

Like all Christians, preachers are called to 'frame and fashion' their 'own life according to the doctrine of Christ' so that they 'may be made an example', not only 'in word but 'in manner of life'. The message has to be in some sense *embodied*, and that can happen only as we 'dwell in Him, and He in us'. (See the 'Ordination of Deaconesses' and the Communion Service in the Methodist *Book of Offices*.) Only when that is happening among those who profess and call themselves Christians, only when we have ourselves abandoned all false 'religion', dare we expect the nations to come to the Lord '*from the ends of the earth*' and say to Him, '*Our fathers have inherited nought but lies*' (verse 19).

17^{1-4}: The indelible sin of Judah

The time has come for Judah to learn once and for all the character of her Lord; in face of His wrath she will even be glad to get out of her devastated land.

17^1. '*pen of iron*'. An instrument with '*the point of a diamond*' which was used to make inscriptions on a '*table*' (tablet) of rock or metal; cf. Job 19^{24}.

'*horns*'. These were projections on the corners of the 'altars'.

17^2. '*Asherim*'. The Hebrew plural of 'asherah'. A sacred pole was set up as a symbol of fertility beside the altar of the goddess Asherah. In popular thought she was confused with Anath and Astarte. (See commentary on 7^{18}.) It seems to have been quite common in the popular belief of the time to regard her as the wife of the Lord!

17^3. '*mountain in the field*'. This is really part of the sentence in verse 2. Read 'by the green trees upon the high hills, upon the mountains in the open country. I will give thee thy substance . . .'.

(This prose paragraph is not included in the *LXX*. With verses 3-4, cf. 15^{13-14}.)

The '*heart*' of the people is corrupt, and inevitably their religion is corrupted through and through. Even the young have been accustomed to serving strange gods. But soon they may have to serve strange people in a foreign land.

Once more the prophet's concern is with the '*heart*' (cf. verse 9). If the heart is wrong, worship cannot be right. Worship without repentance, worship without loyal love to God, simply writes people's sin deeper and deeper into their 'hearts', that is into their very selves, their thinking and feeling and desires (cf. 1 Cor 13^{1-3}). The gospel is that, instead of sin, the law

of God can be written in our hearts, so that we become able
to do His will as spontaneously as we once did our own. So
we pray

> *Write Thy new name upon my heart,*
> *Thy new, best name of love.*   (*MHB* 550; cf. 713)

17⁵⁻¹³: The wisdom of the Lord

Those who trust in human strength cannot come to any good,
but those whose faith is in the Lord will live when the time of
testing comes.

17⁵. '*maketh flesh his arm*'. This is parallel to '*trusteth in man*'
and means much the same—relies and depends on human
powers.

17⁷. Follow *RV*m.

17⁸. '*careful*'. Better 'anxious', full of care.

17¹⁰. '*I try the reins*'. See commentary on **11²⁰**. The Lord puts
our innermost longings to the test.

17¹². '*sanctuary*'. Used here in the sense of 'refuge'.

17¹³. '*written in the earth*'. Better 'in the dust', a great difference
from being engraved on a tablet with a diamond (verse 1).

The man who '*maketh flesh his arm*' does so precisely because
his '*heart*' has departed '*from the Lord*' (verse 5). The '*flesh*' is
human nature as it is turned away from God, and dependence
on human powers of muscle and intelligence is a turning away
from the only worthy Object of our faith. The man who turns
away from Him is cutting himself off from the '*fountain
of living waters*', and he becomes like a dwarf juniper shrub
that withers away in the wilderness where there is no moisture
(verse 6, cf. 2¹³). The description of the consequences of faith
in man and faith in God in Psalm 1 is dependent on verses
5-8 (cf. also Mt 7²⁴⁻⁷, Ps 146, Isa 40³¹). Anyone who trusts
in himself, in his own cleverness or character, is relying on
something that is 'desperately corrupt' (*RSV* of verse 9);

like people who trust in their ill-gotten wealth, he is guilty
of moral stupidity (verse 11). To turn away from the Lord
is to choose death and not life. His Temple is '*a glorious throne,
set on high from the beginning*' and He alone is the '*hope of
Israel*' (verses 12-13; cf. Ps 90[1]).

The 'heart' must be in a completely unhealthy state so long
as we are turned away from God, who alone understands it
(verses 5, 9, 10). Miserable is the man who has nothing to
fall back on but his own 'unconquerable soul': happy is the
man who knows how to trust God and so bring forth the
fruit of the Spirit (cf. verse 8). Christ must dwell in the heart
by faith, to make all well within, to bring about a new creation
of disposition and character, so that we may be filled with all
the fulness of God (cf. Mk 7[21]).

Jeremiah cannot trust his own heart and mind—they are
open to the searching judgement of God. But he can trust
God, who alone is wise and just (verse 10), who alone is life
(verse 13; cf. Jn 4[14], 7[37-9]), and who alone is to be praised
(verse 14). That is why his name is not written in the sand
while those of the false prophets were. And how unjust it is to
think of him merely as the doleful prophet. This poem shows
that he knows where true joy is to be found—in the exacting
life of faith (verses 7-8).

17[14-18]: Let me never be confounded

Because he has never himself desired the coming of the ruin
about which he has to go on warning the people of Judah,
the prophet asks that he may be given faithfulness, and that
the Lord will deal with his persecutors.

17[16]. Follow *RSV* here: 'I have not pressed thee to send evil,
nor have I desired the day of disaster.'

17[18]. '*double*'. See comment on **16[18]**.

Jeremiah puts no confidence in his own powers: healing,
salvation and deliverance can only come to him as a gift
from the Lord (verse 14). What does give him confidence is
the knowledge that he is not a prophet by his own choice;
he has not thrust himself forward, he did not hurl himself into

a position of prominence, and he speaks in the sight of God at all times, with proper reverence and obedience (verse 16). Despite all his suffering, and all his fear, he has God for his '*refuge in the day of evil*' (verse 17). But since God's gifts are truly gifts, and not things to which anyone has a right, it is clear that deliverance is a thing to be prayed for. It will not come automatically. But the people of Judah do not believe that disaster is coming and will not turn and pray. They are treating God's warnings as empty threats which will never be carried out. Jeremiah has no pleasure in speaking of the day of doom, day in day out. Since he knows that God's purpose is fixed, he can only ask that God may act soon (verse 18).

Some preachers may be inclined to point to verse 18 as a good example of an un-Christian attitude to one's enemies. But consider the second verse of the British national anthem which begins, 'O Lord our God arise, Scatter her enemies . . .'. Is the only way of loving our enemies to pray, 'Father, forgive them, for they know not what they do'? Indeed, has anyone the right to offer that prayer, except the Lord Jesus, and those who pray in His name? No one in his senses could take pleasure in warning the enemies of the God of love about His judgement, yet no one who is aware that what he says is before God's face can ignore the truth that the triumph of God's love must involve the annihilation of all that is evil, in us and in our fellow men. Is that annihilation not a part of what we ask for when we pray, 'Thy kingdom come'? If we love our neighbour we do not desire his destruction (verse 16). But if we are hungering and thirsting for righteousness we know that a terrible fate awaits those who persist in refusing God's love, and those who cause His little ones to stumble. Therefore we cannot be silent.

17¹⁹⁻²⁷: The Sabbath

The Lord instructs the prophet to stand in the city gates and remind Judah of the law concerning the Sabbath. If they obey this law, Jerusalem will become a centre of true worship for the whole land, but if they disobey the city will be destroyed.

17¹⁹. '*the gate of the children of the people*'. Possibly the 'Benjamin' gate (cf. *RSV*).

17²¹. Follow *RV*m.

Some commentators believe that this passage must be later than Jeremiah, but, as it stands, it is the first of a group of three signs (cf. 18¹⁻¹², 19¹⁻⁵¹). The passage is sometimes compared with Nehemiah 13¹⁵⁻²², but the emphasis there is different. In *Jeremiah* the people's attitude to the Sabbath is a symptom of the attitude they are taking towards the covenant which God gave them in the time of *Moses* (verses 22-3, cf. 11¹⁻¹⁷). Their bull-headed stubbornness, their complete refusal to accept the Torah (the '*instruction*' of the Lord, verse 23) is to be seen in their refusal to '*hallow the sabbath day*' (verse 24, cf. Ex 20⁸, 31¹⁶, Deut 5¹²⁻¹⁵). The prophet is instructed to secure the greatest possible publicity for his message; a city '*gate*' (verse 19) was a place where one could always be sure of a good open-air meeting, and he is to speak to the '*kings of Judah, and all Judah, and all the inhabitants of Jerusalem*'. Emphasis on the joy of keeping the sabbath as part of the response of a holy people to its covenant-God is also found in later prophets (see Ezek 20¹²⁻²⁰, Isa 56²⁻⁸, 58¹³⁻¹⁴).

Harm has been done, and can still be done, by those who identify the Sabbath, the last day of the week, with the Lord's Day, the first day of the week. But, just as the attitude of the Jew to the Sabbath may be a symptom of his attitude to the covenant of God, so the Christian's attitude to the Lord's Day may be a symptom of his whole attitude to the Giver of the new covenant. The way in which we use Sunday is a part of a whole relationship of obedience and faith towards Him— or of a relationship of rebellion and unbelief. It is part of our stewardship of our time, all of which belongs to God, and it has even greater significance in days when men are beginning to talk about 'the problem of leisure'. The welfare and stability of the whole community (cf. verse 25) depend on an understanding that all our times are in God's hand.

18¹⁻¹²: The Gospel of the second chance

God shows the prophet, in a potter's workshop, that clay which goes wrong in the working can be turned to a different use. So, if a nation repents, God is able to withdraw the punishment He threatened, and if a nation rebels, He can withdraw the blessing He promised. Yet Judah refuses to repent.

18¹. Probably an editorial heading (cf. **11¹, 14¹**).

18². '*house*'. The potter's workshop.

18³. '*wheels*'. The potter worked with two stone discs (cf. Ecclus 38²⁹⁻³⁰). These were attached to an axle so that, as the larger wheel was turned with his foot, the upper one also turned and his hands were free to shape the clay.

It is not the clay's helplessness (cf. Rom 9²⁰) that matters here, but the clay's malleability. Though the potter's first attempt fails, the clay remains workable, and so can still be made into something useful. But with Judah it is different: it is beginning to look as if she is unworkable clay and she will hear no plea to turn (verse 11).

Jeremiah is aware of the pressing of the Potter's fingers on his own life. Verses 7 and 9 recall what was said to him in chapter 1, and since the time when he became conscious of his calling (1⁵), the prophet has found that the Lord's touch upon him has always been nicely adjusted to his own behaviour. He is not made yet, but he is being made. Since it is clear from his own experience that God's resource and patience are inexhaustible, he has every reason to believe that for the people of Judah also there could be hope of a reformation. They could still become a vessel fit to carry God's purpose to the nations. But they will not: instead they say, 'We will follow our own plans' (verse 12 in *RSV*). Indeed (cf. 19¹⁰⁻¹¹), they are less like malleable clay than a brittle flask that must be shattered and '*that cannot be made whole again*'.

The good news is that even a spoiled vessel is still in the Potter's hands, and His 'love will never come to an end' (1 Cor 13⁸ in *NEB*). These verses in *Jeremiah* are a valuable corrective to some of the ways in which Paul's writing about the Potter (Rom 9¹⁹⁻²³) have been interpreted. It is true that 'the potter can do what he likes with the clay' (Rom 9²¹ in *NEB*), but when the Potter is God we know that His 'property is always to have mercy'. He always keeps His end in view,

G

and His changing methods are always perfectly adapted to
that end. So long as the clay remains in a workable condition,
He will go on working with it and will not discard it. (This
of course is not to deny that the clay will not remain workable
for ever—the point that is implicit in 19¹⁻¹⁵.) Man is not
'passive' (cf. *MHB* 572), but living, clay which is able to
respond to the Potter by 'turning' (cf. verse 8). When he does
that, then the Potter 'repents', that is, He adjusts His approach
to this change in the material (cf. 26³, ¹³, ¹⁹). The clay that is
'*marred*' can be '*made*' again, always as seems '*good to the potter*' (verse 4).

There are three elements in the situation: the potter, the
wheel and the clay. The Potter is always at work (cf. Jn 5¹⁷,
6²⁹); His wheel is our environment, the pattern of world
events, and it is always in His control—His foot is on the
lower disc; the clay is ourselves, and He has created us so that
we are workable. No one can become unworkable except
by his own deliberate choice. We must pray that God may
take us and our society, the world in which we live, and re-make
us, before we harden beyond all change (cf. 2 Cor 5¹⁷). No
one is going to deny that 'the potter can do what he likes with
the clay', but what in fact He does is to *become* clay in order
that we may become children of God.

> *He laid His glory by,*
> *He wrapped Him in our clay . . .*
> *To bring our vileness near,*
> *And make us all divine . . .*   (*MHB* 142)

If, despite that, we choose ourselves to go on to the point
where we cease to be workable, it is hardly logical to accuse
the Potter of being despotic and arbitrary. God is not a
monstrous, impersonal machine that deals out salvation and
damnation from a production line: He is the Potter, always at
work, and the last thing He wills is that any of His clay should
end up useless on the scrapheap of the universe. God is free
to do as He pleases, to 'be Himself', and He has shown that
being Himself means being the God of our salvation.

The fact that Paul is skating over thin ice in chapter 9
of Romans should not be allowed to mislead us here. Jeremiah,
at any rate, is not concerned to proclaim a doctrine of fatalism.
He wants Judah to listen to the good news of a second chance
—but they will not (cf. Ezek 18³²).

18¹³⁻¹⁷: An unnatural crime

Nature is constant. But Israel is unfaithful, and therefore what was once the Land of Promise will become a byword among the nations.

18¹⁴. '*the rock of the field*'. This should be 'the crags of Sirion' (cf. *RSV*). 'Sirion' is the Phoenician name for Mount Hermon, (cf. Deut 3⁹). It is impossible to imagine a time when there would be no snow on the summit of Mount Hermon.

18¹⁵. '*vanity*'. They have offered sacrifices to 'nonentity', to false gods who are mere emptiness.

18¹⁶. '*hissing*'. This indicates astonishment, not contempt or hate.

18¹⁷. Follow *RV*m here.

In 8⁴⁻⁷, the inconstancy of God's people is contrasted with the dependability of migratory birds. Here the contrast is with the 'everlasting snows' and the perennial cold mountain streams (verse 14). God's people are completely undependable: they will not keep to the good way (cf. 6¹⁶) appointed by their Creator and Lord, but go off on tracks of their own which will lead them straight to disaster (verses 15-16).

All nature follows the laws of its Maker. But man is an *un*-natural creature, since he flouts his Maker's instructions and disregards his Master's voice. It would hardly be surprising if God always showed us His back and not His face (*RV*m of verse 17). But instead, He has shown us His glory in the face of Jesus Christ, and in Jesus Christ we see the man made in the image of God. What we see in our selves is not real 'human nature', since we have got into such an 'unnatural' state, but we can see our real human nature in Him. He is therefore both our Judge and our Saviour. He is completely dependable, far more dependable than even the 'eternal' hills. He is the water of life, far more refreshing and trustworthy than the clearest of mountain streams. We do well to lift up our eyes to the hills, to listen to what 'all nature says', to look at the birds and consider the lilies of the field, under

His guidance. For He alone can interpret what they have to say; they still proclaim the faithfulness of God which is a rebuke to our inconstancy and 'little faith'.

18¹⁸⁻²³: Plots against Jeremiah

Now the religious leaders have started to plot against him, so the prophet asks the Lord to let the threatened blow fall.

18¹⁸. *'devise devices'*. Conspire or 'make plots' (*RSV*).

18²⁰. *'soul'*. A man's 'soul' was his life (cf. verse 22).

18²¹. *'slain of death'*. Probably means 'killed by plague'.

18²². *'a troop'*. Better, 'the marauder' (*RSV*).

Verse 18 is a prose introduction to this poem. These priests, wise men and prophets know how to hurt Jeremiah: even worse than their readiness to *'smite him with the tongue'*— and 'calling names' *can* hurt—is the fact that they also do *'not give heed to any of his words'*. Only the Lord is willing to listen to him (see verses 18-19). All the religious leaders are anxious to see Jeremiah out of the way. Although he has kept on interceding for their welfare, it now seems clear that they will not believe that God is wakeful unless destruction comes. Therefore the prophet will strive no more to avert it (cf. 17¹⁸ and commentary there).

It is important to observe that *'the priest'*, *'the wise'* and *'the prophet'* are all servants of the Word, above everything else. It is partly because so much has been given to them, and because they have so flagrantly refused to give what is required of them, that the prophet of the Lord sees them as God's arch-enemies and bursts out into this bitter imprecation (cf. Ps 69, 109, 137). There are still things that are *'vile'* as well as those that are *'precious'* in the prophet (cf. 15¹⁹), and he bursts out against those who have so grossly betrayed their calling, as Martin Luther and John Milton were to burst out in similar circumstances centuries later. It needs all the energy of Christ to save us from the harmful kind of 'righteous inidgnation' and make us able to overcome evil with good (cf.

Rom 12¹⁴, ¹⁷⁻²¹). If we will not let God *'forgive'* or *'blot out'* the trespasses of His enemies, how can we expect him to blot out our own (cf. verse 23; Mt 6¹⁵)? And we must take heart from the knowledge that even when men will not listen to us, God will (cf. verses 18-19).

It is when preachers and others who are regarded as religious leaders forget that they are servants of the Word that disaster comes near to the Church, and to the community in which the Church should be witnessing. When we forget that we are servants of the Word, we may be guilty of provoking those who are faithful to something near blasphemy.

19¹⁻¹⁵: A smashed pot

The prophet is to buy an earthenware flask and then go, with representatives of the people and of the priests, to the valley of ben-Hinnom. There he is to tell them that, when God has dealt with those who are worshipping false gods, the valley will be re-named 'Valley of Slaughter'. He must then break the flask, to demonstrate that the Lord will so break His people that it will be impossible to put them together again.

19¹. *'bottle'*. An earthenware jar (cf. 1 Kings 14³).
    'elders of the priests'. Probably the heads of priestly families.

19². Follow *RV*m.

19⁴. *'estranged'*. Desecrated, by offering sacrifice *'unto other gods'*.

19⁵. *'to burn'*. They were burnt to death, not branded.

19⁷. Notice *RV*m. The word is a play on the Hebrew word for 'jar'.

19⁸. *'hissing'*. See commentary on 18¹⁶.

19⁹. *'straitness'*, i.e. distress. *'straiten'*, i.e. afflict.

19¹¹. Follow *RV*m.

19¹². '*as Topheth*'. Topheth had already been defiled deliberately (cf. 2 Kings 23¹⁰). Now the holy city itself is to suffer the same fate.

19¹³. '*which are defiled*', because they have had sacrifices to '*all the host of heaven*', the whole gamut of astral deities, offered upon their '*roofs*'; cf. **32²⁹**.

This solemn symbolic act caused a great sensation in official quarters and seems to have stung Jeremiah's opponents into open action against him (cf. **20¹⁻²**). The word of the Lord is still the same, but because it is now expressed in dramatic action as well as in speech, men cease to scoff. They react swiftly. They have filled the valley with '*the blood of innocents*' (verse 4) and have been ready to throw their '*sons in the fire for burnt offerings unto Baal*', so it is not surprising that they fear an acted word. They have long been scoffing at the same word when it was given to them in the words of Jeremiah, but action is something different. It was believed by the prophet and everyone else that such an action was the beginning of the fulfilment of what it signified, and that it actually 'triggered off' the thing represented.

The idea that to sacrifice one's son, and especially one's first-born son, was the most effective sacrifice of all took a long time to die in Israel. It lasted long after the days of Abraham (cf. Mic 6⁷, 2 Kings 3²⁷, 16³, 21⁶). Josiah tried to make any repetition of the practice impossible for the future (2 Kings 23¹⁰), but the custom was revived (cf. Ezek 16²⁰, 20²⁶). Jeremiah's protest, here and in 7³¹⁻³, is one of the first signs of a developing revulsion against the practice (cf. commentary on **32³⁵**, below). The prophet regards this type of sacrifice as a shocking reversion to barbarous heathen customs and declares that it will lead to the destruction of Jerusalem (verse 8). Those who have offered to Moloch (32³⁵—this is more accurate than '*Baal*' in verse 5) sacrifices that even the Lord has never required of them, will find, when their punishment comes, that they will give way to cannibalism also, and will eat their relatives and friends (verse 9). Once again the prophet is instructed to secure the widest possible publicity for his warning (verses 1, 14); it was most unusual for a man to be seen doing woman's work and carrying a jar (cf. Mk 14¹³).

There are times when the Servant of the Lord is not required to 'cry, nor lift up, nor cause his voice to be heard in the street' (Isa 42²). But there are other times when the Church must use the most effective methods of making the world listen. Any community that ignores the covenant of God is not very far from barbarism, and especially the kind of barbarism that masquerades as up-to-dateness and contemporary enlightenment. Preachers may recall happenings not very long ago in Nazi Germany and Stalin's Russia, in Hiroshima and Hungary. But we have also to ask ourselves what is God's judgement on a world in which we are ready to sacrifice the '*blood of innocents*' to drunken drivers on our roads, to nuclear weapon tests, and to selfishness in the economic affairs of the nations (cf. 2 Kings 6²⁸⁻³⁰). There is still a desperate need for that faithful dealing between man and man which is the fruit of a proper acceptance of God's covenant; the world needs badly those who 'do justly', 'love mercy' and 'walk humbly with' God (Mic 6⁸).

20¹⁻¹⁸: In the stocks

Jeremiah is flogged and put in the stocks overnight. When the prophet is released, he warns the chief of the Temple guard that he will be among those who are taken as prisoners to Babylon when Jerusalem falls.

Jeremiah complains to the Lord. He has become a laughing-stock.

20¹. '*chief officer*'. Probably the head of the Temple guard (cf. Lk 22⁵²).

20². '*the upper gate of Benjamin*'. This is a gate in the Temple, presumably on the north side of the compound (cf. commentary on 1¹).

20³. See *RV*m (cf. verse 10).

20⁴. '*Babylon*'. This is the first passage in *Jeremiah*, as we have it, where the 'foe from the north' is named. The incident is not dated, but this is an indication that it is almost certainly after the Egyptian retreat from Carchemish (see Introduction).

20⁶. '*prophesied falsely*'. Another indication of the close connection between priests and prophets. By this action in punishing the prophet, Pashhur is telling the people that the madman from Anathoth is not to be taken seriously, and so Pashhur is a false prophet who does not know the way of the Lord.

20⁷. From this point on, the chapter is in verse. Editors may have included this poem here because of the link between verse 10 and verse 3.

'*laughing-stock*'. The mockery that he has endured in the stocks is no new thing (cf. Lam 3¹⁴).

'*O Lord, thou hast deceived me*'. Cf. **15¹⁸**. The prophet roundly accuses God of being a liar (see commentary on **15¹⁰⁻²¹**). It was believed that He could put both true and false messages into the mouth of a prophet (cf. Deut 13²⁻³). God may deliberately mislead people for His own purposes (cf. 1 Kings 22¹⁹⁻²⁴)—or so it was thought, and there are moments when Jeremiah is inclined to think they may be right. This is poetry, not dogma!

20¹⁰. '*halting*'. Better, 'fall' (*RSV*).

20¹³. '*soul*'. Better, 'life'.

20¹⁶. '*cities*'. Sodom and Gomorrah (Gen 19).
'*shouting*'. Follow *RV*m.

Pashhur is not mentioned in 29²⁵⁻⁶ and he may have been among those deported (verse 6) in 598 BC. This would mean that **19¹-20⁶** deal with the days shortly before the rebellion of Jehoiakim (cf. note on verse 4 above). The Temple official who has made the prophet a prisoner will himself become a prisoner—in Babylon; the one who has terrorised God's spokesman, will himself be terrorised, and with him those to whom he has '*prophesied falsely*' (verse 6). Pashhur's end will be death in exile (cf. Amos 7¹⁷). Meanwhile, his nickname will be 'Terror-on-every-side', and this name will have its fulfilment.

The poem (verses 7-18) moves swiftly through moods of sorrow and bitter protest, of hope and black despair. The writer never aspired to be a prophet; his own feelings were pushed aside from the outset (**1⁷**). It is useless for him to try to keep quiet; the word will out (verse 9; cf. Amos 3⁸). He feels as if his innermost self has been invaded and overpowered ('*deceived*' in verse 7 means 'seduced; cf. Ezek 14⁹). And yet he has to go back again in faith to the One who has made his life a misery, for He is, after all, the God and Saviour of the needy (verse 13). But there are certainly times when he curses the day he was born (verses 14-18; cf. Job 3¹⁻¹⁰ which is probably based on these verses).

Probably the most helpful feature of this remarkable passage is its honesty. It can help us, not because it is repository of sound doctrine on the 'problem of suffering', but because it shows in poetry that even a faithful servant of God could feel, as we do now, the frustration that arises because we cannot know as we are known. God is in heaven: we are on earth. His ways are not our ways; His thoughts are not our thoughts. And when the pressure on us becomes heavy, we are always liable to scream because we are being hurt very badly. The picture we are given here of this man, smarting from the flogging, haggard, half-frozen, craving sleep, ready to cry, 'My God, my God, why hast thou forsaken me?' surely has something to say to us all, and perhaps especially to those who say 'God let me down badly; I can't believe in Him'. In this poem we see how others have had to say:

> '*My faith burns low, my hope burns low;*
> *Only my heart's desire cries out in me . . .*' (*MHB* 94)

others have had to wrestle with the 'Traveller unknown', and be badly injured, before they could assert, with a dawning joy still mixed with resentment,

> '*All helplessness, all weakness, I*
> *On Thee alone for strength depend.*' (*MHB* 339)

The God who spared not His own Son never promises His servants freedom from trouble or sorrow, or persecution, or from bewilderment and enveloping doubt. He simply promises to be with them—always.

We have need in a Christian hymnbook for a section on 'Temptation and Conflict', as well as one on 'Trustfulness and Peace'. We must beware of presenting the Kingdom of God as if it were a sort of 'Welfare State'; its citizens are a company of witnesses. The Greek for 'to witness' is *martyreo*, and every witness is in some sense a 'martyr' (cf. 1 Pet 2[19-25]). We are privileged to be allowed this intimate and vivid glimpse of a part of the process by which God made Jeremiah into His man (cf. 1 Cor 1[26-31]). God's children have to learn, often painfully, that they must not become guilty of treachery to their Lord by keeping silence when He wishes them to speak, no matter what it may cost them. It is hard to 'fight and not to heed the wounds', especially when they seem to be the result of our General's negligence, or incompetence, or callousness: but this is a real part of serving Him as He deserves to be served—with absolute faith, and the 'love that never falters'.

21[1-14]: An answer for the king

When Zedekiah asks for the prophet's advice about the attack that Nebuchadrezzar is making on Judah.

21[1]. '*Pashhur the son of Malchiah*'. A different Pashhur from '*the son of Immer*' in the previous chapter (cf. 20[1]). But the similarity of the names may have led the editors to group these two incidents together, in spite of the fact that we are now dealing with the period about 17 years after that of chapter 20.

'*Zephaniah*'. Probably the 'second priest' mentioned in 52[24]; cf. 37[3]. In 29[24-9] it appears that this Zephaniah had responsibility for the policing of the Temple, but was more sympathetic to Jeremiah than the Pashhur of chapter 20.

21[2]. '*go up from us*'. Withdraw from besieging the city, raise the siege.

21[9]. '*falleth away*', i.e. surrenders, goes over to the enemy.
    '*for a prey*'. The only plunder he will get from the fighting will be his own survival, and that by the skin of his teeth.

21[12]. '*in the morning*'. Without delay, (although it is also true that the usual time for the royal court of justice was in the forenoon). Cf. Psalm 72[2], Isaiah 9[7], 32[1].

21[13]. '*inhabitant*'. This is feminine in the Hebrew (see *RV*m); Judah is the fallen Bride of the Lord.

'*of the rock*'. Follow *RV*m. God is against Zion, 'the rock of the plain'. The details of the verse are rather obscure, but the general meaning seems to be that God will punish those in Judah and Jerusalem who think that they are in an impregnable position.

The '*Chaldeans*' (verses 4, 9) are the people we should call 'Babylonians'. The rulers of the new empire came from Chaldea in the south of Babylonia.

Verses 12-14 are in verse. Verses 1-10 may be another version of the incident reported in **37³⁻¹⁰**, which apparently belongs to the time just before the fall of Jerusalem in 587 B C. Hitherto it has usually been the false prophets who have been officially approached as experts in intercession, but now Zedekiah approaches Jeremiah. The king is hoping for another of the Lord's '*wondrous works*', though his '*peradventure*' (verse 2) may indicate that he has good reason to fear something very different in this prophet's reply. And so it is. The only choice that is left to the King of Judah is between death in the city or life outside (verses 8-9). Things are not what they used to be in the days of Isaiah and Hezekiah and Sennacherib; this time it will be the Jerusalemites who will fall victims to plague (verse 6), and not the besieging army. This is the '*fruit*' of despising God's warnings; Judah must reap the disaster she has sown.

Zedekiah's is the wrong kind of assurance—the belief that God will go on working miracles on our behalf, no matter what we do. But his assurance is moving towards a mood of disillusion and it would be difficult not to be affected by his '*peradventure*' (verse 2; *RSV* has 'perhaps'). But however affected and sympathetic the prophet may be, it is his responsibility to speak the word of the Lord. Yes, God will deliver Zedekiah, but it will be a deliverance of him '*into the hand of Nebuchadrezzar king of Babylon*' (verse 7). Even when men are reaping the '*fruit*' of their '*doings*' (cf. verse 14) there is still an opportunity to choose between '*the way of life and the way of death*' (verse 8) and it is the Lord who permits us the choice. Even on the brink of destruction, when the universe seems to be crashing in ruin around us, we are still required and called to be obedient to Him. Even then, and this is the gospel, the Lord offers us the opportunity to obey, and the strength to obey, if we will

accept it. It may be that the crash cannot be averted, that the
heavens still may fall, but those who obey will find, beyond
the breakdown of every worldly thing in which we trust,
the truth of the good news— '*he shall live, and his life shall be
unto him for a prey*'. Our Lord showed us in Gethsemane that
the way forward that God wills for us may lie in a real acceptance of the very thing from which we desire so earnestly to
escape; it may be only when we have 'surrendered' to the
enemy that He sends, only when we have 'died', that we shall
find life beginning again.

If we think that we are secure (cf. verse 13), we are still on
the wrong side of that word '*peradventure*'.

22¹-23⁸: The royal family

The house of David is urged to help the oppressed and to
enforce justice, otherwise the royal line will be brought to an
end.

22¹. '*Go down*'. This may suggest that the prophet received
the message whilst he was in the Temple. He would have to
go down to the palace.

22⁶⁻⁷. A section in verse. '*Gilead*' and '*Lebanon*' were widely
known as richly forested areas.

22¹⁰⁻¹². A brief oracle in verse on 'him that goeth away',
i.e. '*Shallum*' (Jehoahaz, see *RV*m), the successor of '*the dead*'
Josiah. Shallum had gone '*forth out of this place*' as an exile
into Egypt, and there he died (cf. 2 Kings 23²⁸⁻³³, 1 Chron
3¹⁵).

22¹³⁻¹⁹. Another oracle in verse, this time concerning
Jehoiakim who had been put in Shallum's place by the Egyptians (cf. 1 Kings 21¹⁷⁻²⁴, 2 Kings 23³³⁻⁵).

22¹⁵. '*shalt thou reign*'. That is 'do you think you are a king?'
(cf. *RSV*).

22¹⁷. Follow *RV*m—'dishonest gain'.
'*innocent blood*'. Cf. 26²³.

22¹⁸. *'They shall not lament'*. Neither relatives nor subjects will be able to join in the conventional lamentations when he dies.

22¹⁹. This prophecy does not appear to have been fulfilled. See 2 Kings 24⁶.

22²⁰⁻³. An oracle in verse on Jerusalem.

22²⁰. *'Lebanon'*, *'Bashan'* and *'Abarim'* (probably Mount Nebo). These three mountain ranges were in the north, north-east and south-east respectively, on the horizon.

22²¹. *'thy youth'*. Cf. 2². Jerusalem has been disobedient from the outset: Israel was at least obedient at first.
   'prosperity'. This really means 'security' or 'comfort'.

22²². *'feed'*. Read with *RSV*, 'The wind shall shepherd all your shepherds', i.e. the wind will blow, to the dismay of their leaders who will be swept away, gone with the wind.

22²³. *'Lebanon'*. This seems to be used here as a metaphor for Jerusalem; cf. the simile in verse 6.

22²⁴⁻⁷. This prose oracle on Jehoiachin is followed by one in verse (verses 28-30) on the same king. Jehoiachin or *'Coniah'* ruled only for a hundred days; cf. 13¹⁸⁻¹⁹.

22²⁴. *'signet'*. Such a ring was a treasured possession. The idea of the king as the Lord's 'signet' became common in Messianic writings. Haggai deliberately reverses this prophecy in speaking of Zerubbabel (Hag 2²³).

22²⁶. *'mother'*. Nehushta; cf. 13¹⁸ and comment thereon.

22²⁸. ²⁹. Follow *RV*m.

22³⁰. *'childless'*. This is a rather misleading translation. The word probably means 'proscribed' so that there is no heir (cf. Lev 20²⁰, ²¹). No successor of his will ever rule as king. The prophet is telling those who were looking for Coniah's early return from exile that he will not come again. In fact

Coniah's grandson, Zerubbabel, became governor, but not king, of Judah. (See note on verse 24 above.)

23¹. '*shepherds*'. Again these are rulers, and the flock is not theirs, but the Lord's.

23². '*visited*', '*visit*'. Because they have not 'attended' to the Lord's flock, the Lord will 'attend' to them in no uncertain manner (cf. *RSV*).

23⁵. '*Branch*'. Another Messianic term; cf. note above on **22²⁴**. There is to be a new 'shoot' (*RV*m) from the dead-looking stump of the Vine, which is Israel (cf. **33¹⁵⁻¹⁶, 2²¹, 12¹⁰**). This is a vivid metaphor as anyone will agree who has seen the old vine stock which is apparently dead, and then the new shoot bursting vigorously out of it when the spring weather comes.

23⁶. '*The Lord is our righteousness*'. There is a play here on the name Zedekiah which means 'the Lord is my righteousness'.

23⁷⁻⁸. Cf. **16¹⁴⁻¹⁵** and comment thereon.

This collection of prose and verse oracles concerning the kings of Judah may have been placed here because the editors felt that it follows suitably on **21¹¹⁻¹⁴**—in fact, **21¹¹** may have been intended as the title to the whole collection: 'Concerning the royal house of Judah'. Underlying the whole group of sayings is the belief which made the prophets' conception of monarchy so different from the governing idea in most ancient societies —the belief that rulers of the house of David must obey the Lord.

Some of the prophet's disappointment with Zedekiah is apparent in **23⁶**. The king's name means 'The Lord my righteousness', but he does not fulfil the promise of that name, so Jeremiah invents the name '*the Lord* our *righteousness*' (see *RV*m of **23⁶**) for the Messianic figure who will one day come. He will not make a merely conventional claim to have righteousness as his own royal perquisite, but he will be the fulfilment of all that the Lord can do through His chosen prince. Through him the righteousness of God will be mediated to the whole people; they shall all know the Lord's righteousness, from the greatest to the least. When the Lord's Messiah comes to live up to this name, Judah and Israel will live together in security. Their return from exile will throw into the shade even the wonder of the Exodus from Egypt in the days of Moses (23⁷⁻⁸).

A list of this last group of kings of Judah may be helpful at this stage:

608 B C. Josiah killed at Megiddo.
Jehoahaz (Shallum) succeeds Josiah.
Jehoiakim succeeds Jehoahaz who was deposed by the Pharaoh Necho.
597 B C. Jehoiachin (or Jeconiah or Coniah) succeeds Jehoiakim who had died.
Zedekiah succeeds Jehoiachin who was deposed by Nebuchadrezzar.
586 B C. Zedekiah is defeated and deposed by Nebuchadrezzar.

Jeremiah solemnly asserted that none of this family would ever sit on the throne of David again. Jehoiachin had children (cf. '*seed*' in 22²⁸, 1 Chron 3¹⁷⁻¹⁸, Mt 1¹²); there even exist cuneiform tablets discovered at Babylon listing the rations which were granted to the captive Jehoiachin and his children. But Jeremiah was right; it was true that '*no man of his seed*' was to rule as king '*any more in Judah*' (22³⁰). The Messiah who came to command men to seek God's kingdom and His righteousness above everything else (cf. Mt 6³³), and who made it possible for us to do so, was lifted up on a Cross outside the city wall (cf. Jn 18³³⁻⁷).

It is not often necessary in these days for a preacher to stand before princes in the way that the prophets did. But the principles on which good leadership rests remain the same, whether men are governed by elected governments, dictators, business cartels, trade unions, technicians, or any other kind of authority. Christians should be standing before such powerful groups, wherever they hold sway, to remind them of God's kingdom and His righteousness. All authority is responsible to God and must show a proper love for Him and for the neighbour. The prophet condemns kings who are in a wrong relationship to the Lord (22⁹) and who are in a wrong relationship to His flock (22¹³). Conversely Josiah is honoured, not because of his 'reformation', but because he 'knew' the Lord and this knowledge was apparent in his attitude to defenceless people (22¹⁵⁻¹⁶). The same principles apply to those in authority today, because the Lord is 'righteous'. He cares for the defenceless, the poor, the needy, the humble, the hungry, the oppressed. When the nations are judged, it will matter little whether they had the first nuclear weapon or were the first to send astronauts to the moon; what will matter is whether they '*judged the cause of the poor and needy*' (22¹⁶; cf. Mt 25³¹⁻⁴⁶).

The preacher will recognize that the implications of these paragraphs are not confined to a Coronation year, or Christian Citizenship Sunday or some such special occasion; here in the dark days when he is about to '*destroy*' and '*overthrow*', the Lord is at work also '*to build, and to plant*' (1¹⁰) for a future even more wonderful than the prophet could imagine. The key words are '*judgement and righteousness*', '*deliver*', '*the cause of the poor and needy*', '*judgement and justice*, (22³, ¹⁶, 23⁵). 'Judgement' is '*mishpat*' (see commentary on 9²⁴), and 'justice' is a synonym for 'righteousness'. We know that the Lord is 'righteous' because He 'delivers' those who are 'poor and needy'—He is their Saviour (cf. Ps 34⁶, 35¹⁰, 40¹⁷. See *TWB*, pp. 202-4 and *NHS*, pp. 68-78 and *passim*). What is implied in 23⁵⁻⁶ becomes explicit in 33¹⁶, where the result of the coming of the 'Branch' or Messiah is '*judgement and righteousness in the land*', and it is the people whom the Lord has '*saved*' through His Messiah who bear the name '*The Lord is our righteousness*' (see commentary below on 33¹⁻²⁶). This prophecy is fulfilled for us when we can say of Christ Jesus, 'he is our righteousness' (1 Cor 1³⁰, *NEB*). Whether we are blessed with leaders who seek first God's righteousness, or we suffer under bad shepherds (cf. 23¹⁻²), we can have a Good Shepherd to rule over us, who is the King of Kings and Lord of Lords.

'To act righteously and to love mercy' is the same thing as 'humbling oneself to walk with God' (cf. Mic 6⁸); to 'know' God is to respond to the demands of our Lord with '*judgement and justice*' (cf. 22¹⁵⁻¹⁶). This is a righteousness which we can learn only by companying with God Himself, a righteousness which involves a special concern with '*the poor and the needy*' (cf. Mt 5²⁰).

> *His only righteousness I show*
> *His saving grace proclaim.* (*MHB* 92)

23⁹⁻⁴⁰: False Prophets

The prophets will be punished, for they are spreading ungodliness. They pretend to be proclaiming the word of the Lord when they are merely relying on their own invention.

23¹⁰. '*swearing*'. Follow *RV*m. '*force*', or 'might' (*RSV*).

23¹⁵. '*wormwood*', '*gall*'. Bitter poisons to put a stop to their doings.

23¹⁷. Notice *RV*m. This is one of the places where it seems that a correct Hebrew text can be recovered by reference to the *LXX*. Cf. verse 33.

23²⁶. '*How long shall this be*'. The Hebrew is obscure. *RSV* has an interesting conjecture, based on the ancient Syriac version, 'How long shall there be lies'.

23³³. '*What burden!*' Follow *RV*m—'Ye are the burden'.

23³⁶. Follow *RV*m.

23³⁹. Follow *RV*m. The Lord is going to lift them up and 'hurl' them away; so He will un-burden Himself of them (cf. verse 33).

Following the collection of oracles about the royal family the editors now include another collection, concerned this time with prophets. The prophets of Judah are worse than those who once prophesied (and perhaps those who are still prophesying) in the northern kingdom of Samaria (verse 13). The prophets are attacked on five main counts: (*a*) they are of bad character, (*b*) they seek their own popularity, (*c*) they confuse their own dreams with the word of God, (*d*) they steal their messages from others, and all these things arise from the fact that (*e*) they have not '*stood in the council of the Lord*' (verse 18).

The true prophet is one who perceives and hears and obeys the word of his Lord (verse 18) because he stands and waits in His presence (cf. **42⁷**). He is changed in himself by that word (verse 9) and he knows what it is to have a '*burden*'. But the false prophets, although they claim to speak for the

H

Lord, are not leading evil-doers to repent but are confirming them in their ways (verses 14, 17). Their powers are misdirected (cf. *'their force is not right'*, verse 10), they have 'lies in the heart' (verse 26 in *RSV*), and they are full of their own importance (verse 25) to such an extent that they lead other people to forget God (verse 27). One might think that God was in the pocket of these hucksters, but in fact He is far away from them (verse 23, cf. **14**[18]). They claim to have a *'burden'* from God, when in reality they themselves are such a burden to Him that He will soon unburden Himself and hurl them all away. These humbugs who are setting their own word in place of the word of the Lord will find that, when they themselves badly need the word of the Lord, they will be left with nothing but their own word (verses 39-40).

The false prophets seem to have brushed aside these criticisms, but no preacher can afford to do that. God's attack in these prophecies is made on official religion that has gone bad—and the rot began with the prophets, the ministers of the word, the preachers. Taking the name of the Lord in vain is seen at its worst, not among conscious blasphemers, but at religious meetings where preachers may hold forth about heavenly things with much assurance and importance—but no knowledge. Once we become spiritually bankrupt we soon fall a pray to time-serving, plagiarising and cant. Irving Babbit has said, 'Where there is no vision . . . the people perish, but where there is sham vision, they perish even faster'. The only Lord who is to be served in preaching is the One whose word is like a fire, or a hammer (verse 29, cf. **20**[9]), the One who leads us to the point where we have to say 'Even if I preach the Gospel, I can claim no credit for it; I cannot help myself; it would be misery to me not to preach. . . . I do it apart from my own choice, I am simply discharging a trust' (1 Cor 9[16-17], *NEB*). Therefore we must beware of 'sham vision'; we must not quench the Spirit through personal enthusiasms and prejudices. We must be on our guard against any bias arising through tradition or contemporary fashions in belief or we may begin to proclaim something other than the gospel—the manifesto of an ecclesiastical party, a man-made thing, an idol.

The place where the preacher receives the word of God is a fellowship, the fellowship of the Church, the communion created and nourished by the Holy Spirit. Unless we continue in that holy fellowship our characters will become worse, we shall seek our own popularity, we shall confuse our own dreams with the word of God, and we shall steal other people's messages, because we can no longer perceive or obey the word of God for ourselves. Jeremiah knew that it was essential for a preacher to be called to be a member of God's '*council*' (verses 18, 22); without the wonderful and costly privilege of being included in God's fellowship-class it was impossible to be a true prophet. The Hebrew word translated as '*council*' is *sodh* and it describes a relationship which is not official and formal but really intimate. But while it is true that God is intimate with His prophets and shares His secrets with them for the sake of all men (cf. Amos 3[7]), it is clear also that the *sodh* is His creation and no one may belong to it except by His invitation (cf. Jn 15[16]). Those who belong to God's '*council*' are there because of a royal summons which takes precedence over everything else (cf. Mk 3[13-14]). Their calling is to 'know' God, to interpret His ways to their fellowmen and to preach to them the good news that the living God is our Saviour and our King (cf. Mk 1[15]).

It is because the Bible knows nothing of a solitary God who keeps Himself to Himself that there can be no such thing as a solitary Christian. This is why it is not impossible for any human being to claim to be in the '*council*' of God. But if the claim is false, the result will be to 'err in vision' and 'stumble in judgement' (Isa 28[7]); because the Lord has not '*sent*' them (see verses 21, 32) they cannot 'expect him to fulfil their word' (Ezek 13[6]). This is the kind of apostolic succession that really matters—the succession of those who are apostled or 'sent' by the Lord, those who can say 'the Lord took me . . . and the Lord said unto me, Go, prophesy . . .' (Amos 7[15]). It is a wonderful thing for any man to belong to this heavenly fellowship meeting (or 'class-meeting') and a wonderful thing to be sent forth from it to bear witness to the living God and His sovereign activity (cf. Mk 4[11], Rev 10[7]). It would also be a wonderful thing if our earthly fellowship-meetings were true reflections of the heavenly *sodh*.

> *The secret of the Lord is theirs . . .*
> *Still to the lowly soul*
> *He doth Himself impart.*   (*MHB* 950)

Where there is this fellowship in which the Lord's promise is fulfilled, it throws up good preachers, journalists who are true prophets, and Christians who go about their apostolic work with joy. (More features of the '*council*' of the Lord who is pleased to make His secret known to men will be seen in Job 15⁸, 29⁴, Ps 25¹⁴, 55¹⁴, 89⁷, 111¹, Prov 3³². There is matter here for Trinity Sunday: God is a 'society', and this is the society He keeps. . . .)

24¹⁻¹⁰: Figs, good and bad

The difference between the people carried off to Babylon and those left behind in Jerusalem is like that between very good figs and rotten ones.

24¹. '*Jeconiah*'. This is Jehoiachin or Coniah who was taken to Babylon with his mother Nehushta in 597 BC (Cf. 2 Kings 24¹⁰⁻¹⁷ and commentary on 22²⁴⁻³⁰).

24². '*first ripe*'. Figs that ripen in June are a great delicacy.

24⁸. '*Egypt*'. This is probably a reference to the group that had gone with ex-king Jehoahaz (cf. 22¹⁰).
'*princes*'. Here probably refers to the 'noblemen' who were Zedekiah's officials.

24⁹. Follow *RV*m.

This message to the people of Jerusalem has a counterpart in a message to the exiles which is in chapter **29**. Notice that both groups are '*set before . . . the Lord*' (verse 1), and it is in His estimation that their futures are good and bad respectively. Far from being secure while their fellows are being punished (cf. Ezek 11¹⁵), the people left in Jerusalem are ripe for destruction. But for the exiles in Babylon there is a good future, since God intends to give them '*a heart to know*' Himself (verse 7; cf. 31³³⁻⁴). See commentary on **29¹⁻³²** for further description of the position of the exiles.

We do not always remember how revolutionary the ideas of the prophets must have seemed to their contemporaries. Most of the people in Judah still assumed that anyone who had to live outside Palestine would have to 'serve other gods' (cf.

1 Sam 26¹⁹), since it was impossible to 'sing the Lord's song in a strange land' (Ps 137⁴). Any country other than the promised land is reckoned to be 'a land that is unclean' (Amos 7¹⁷). From this point of view the disappearance of the state of Judah would mean the disappearance of the worship of the Lord as well. So the people in Judah were saying of the exiles. 'They have gone far from the Lord; to us this land is given for a possession' (*RSV* of Ezek 11¹⁵). But Jeremiah has been shown (see verse 1) that being 'far from the Lord' is not a matter of geography, but of where one's *'heart'* is (cf. Jn 4¹⁹⁻²⁴).

This chapter is a good illustration of the danger of complacence; of piously discerning the work of God in the punishment of other people, while forgetting that we ourselves may be on the brink of disaster (cf. 1 Cor 10¹²). Conversely, it is wrong for those who seem to be in the unfortunate group to give themselves up to despair, forgetting that their trouble may be *'for good'* (verses 5-6; cf. Rom 8²⁸). God may deprive us of false ideas of security, He may set us free from false hopes and standards to which other people are still able to cling, so that we are brought to a place where He may build us up from a new beginning. (Verse 7 is a beautiful bud ready to blossom into all the glory of 31³¹⁻⁷.)

25¹⁻¹⁴: Disobedience means destruction

Here the editors have placed material which has been gathered to serve as a summary of chapters **1-24;** see the phrase *'this book, which Jeremiah hath prophesied'* in verse 13. It also is intended to serve as a preface to the messages about *'all the nations'* which occur at this point in the arrangement of the book which is followed in the *LXX*. (Our English versions follow the Hebrew Bible and incorporate these oracles later in the book—our chapters **46-51.**)

This passage must be considered in conjunction with the account in chapter **36** of how Baruch put the prophecies of Jeremiah into written form. In 605 BC the Pharaoh Necho was driven back from Carchemish on the river Euphrates by Nebuchadrezzar. It was now clear to the prophet that the Chaldeans were the foe from the *'north'*, that the Lord was using them to fulfil the warnings that He had been sending to His people through Jeremiah ever since the time when it became clear that the power of Assyria was at an end. Many nations are about to come under the sway of the Chaldeans. Since Judah has refused to listen to the repeated warnings from the Lord, she also is about to come under their domination for a long, though still limited, period.

25¹. '*the fourth year of Jehoiakim*'. The year in which the Chaldeans drove the Egyptians south from Carchemish.

25³. '*the thirteenth year of Josiah*'. See **1²** and commentary on **1¹⁻³**.

25⁴. '*rising up early*'. Cf. **7²⁵**. This strong metaphor describes God's persistence and urgency in warning His people.

25⁹. Read, 'behold, this is the Lord's word,—I am about to send and take all the tribes of the north and Nebuchadrezzar the King of Babylon, my servant, and I will bring them against this land . . .'.

25¹⁴. Read 'For they, even they (*i.e. the Chaldeans*) shall serve many nations and great kings' (cf. *RV*m).

Here is a reminder of what it must have cost Jeremiah to go on, year after year, obediently passing on an unwelcome message from the Lord. He was a voice crying in the wilderness, not the wilderness of burning rock away from the villages, but a wilderness of contempt, indifference, bewilderment, frustration, loneliness and despair in the midst of his own people. Now the thing that he has feared so long, and feared the more because he was a poet who could visualize it all so clearly, seems certain. His people have left God with no alternative but to use the Chaldean, a terrible instrument, as His servant against them (verse 9). The land will be devastated so that no sign of human occupation is left; the '*sound of the millstones*' will be heard no longer by day, and the '*light of the candle*' will be no more seen there at night (verse 10). The only consolation is that after three score years and ten, beyond the span of a normal human life, the power of the Chaldeans will be brought to an end (verses 11-12).

'*seventy years*' (cf. **29¹⁰**) is a round number; the point is that, although few or none of those who hear the message from God's prophet will live to see it, the end of the Chaldean empire is certain because the Lord rules over all men. Much nonsense would never have been written, and much more would never have been spoken, if only people had understood this, and if only they had accepted the fact that this prophecy was fulfilled, even more precisely than the prophet could have anticipated. The first group of Jews to return from Babylon travelled in 538 B C and the Temple was re-dedicated in Jerusalem in 516 B C, seventy years after the fall of the city.

See also the commentary on chapter **36** below.

25¹⁵⁻³⁸: The cup of wrath

God's judgement is to be executed on all the nations, starting from Jerusalem.

25¹⁸. '*as it is this day*'. A 'footnote' added by a scribe.

25²⁰. '*mingled people*'. The foreigners living in Egypt (cf. Ezek 30⁵).

25²². '*the isle which is beyond the sea*'. Follow *RV*m. The reference is to the coast on the other side of the Mediterranean Sea.

25²³. See commentary on 9²⁶.

25²⁶. Notice *RV*m.

25³¹. '*he will plead with*'. Better 'he will prosecute'.

25³⁴. '*shepherds*', '*principal of the flock*'. Once again the reference is to the rulers of the nation.

25³⁸. Just as a lion deserts his den if it is destroyed, so the Lord will abandon the land of Judah when it is devastated. Cf. *RSV*.

From verse 30 to the end of the chapter (with the exception of verse 33) the Hebrew is in verse. In the prose section (verses 15-29), God is the great King and the prophet is the royal cupbearer at an awful banquet. The nations are His guests, and the only drink to be served is judgement. This has to be taken by everyone. In the poem, God is a lion against whom neither sheep nor shepherd can stand. This Lion of Judah is no mighty champion of His people, but their judge and executioner. The arrangement of the *LXX* suggests that some early Hebrew manuscripts had the oracles which now form our chapters **46-51** at this point (see commentary on verses 1-14 above). This would mean that the arrangement was on the same pattern as in *Isaiah* 1^{1-39} and *Ezekiel*, where oracles on the nations are put in the middle and not at the end of the book. The list of nations in verses 19-26 is linked with the prophecies which are found in chapters **46-51,** and reference should be made to the commentary below on those chapters.

In verses 31-3 we again have evidence that fellowship with God could sometimes mean that a prophet's thought was launched into space, into realms beyond the grasp of his reason or imagination. To this day, even the most acute theologians have never been able to work out the complete significance of the truth that nothing in the universe can survive if God disapproves of it, and its corollary—its amazing and exhilarating corollary—that everything in the universe of which He approves will survive and find fulfilment.

One of the roots of the Church's missionary responsibility is that God is Judge of all the nations (cf. Mt 25^{32}); that is why He instructs us to go 'into all the world' and preach the gospel. For us the whole picture has been changed, because we have a Master who has Himself drunk the bitter cup of God's judgement for us, and for all the nations (cf. Mk. 14^{36}, Jn 18^{11}). He has done this in order that He might offer His people a very different cup (cf. 1 Cor 11^{25-6}, 10^{16}). This 'cup of blessing' is the pledge of the One who has brought in the New Covenant by His death, that He will be present with His people to the end of the age, in order that they may be able to proclaim to all the nations the good news that He is their Judge and their Saviour. The gospel is that everything that denies or obstructs the Kingdom of God is doomed. But this can become *good* news for us only when we accept the Kingdom of God, and obey Him as Lord.

We believe that Thou shalt come to be our Judge:
We therefore pray Thee, help Thy servants, whom Thou hast
redeemed with Thy precious blood.

II. Scenes from the life of Jeremiah. (26¹-45⁵)

26¹⁻²⁴: Jeremiah saved from death

Not long after the death of Josiah, the Lord tells the prophet
to warn the people of Judah that, unless they change their
ways, Jerusalem and the Temple will come to the same end
as Israel's shrine at Shiloh had suffered long ago at the hand
of the Philistines. (The narrative is connected with chapter 7.
See commentary.)

26¹⁰. '*princes*'. Important officials, not members of the royal
family.

26¹⁸. Notice *RV*m.

26²³. '*graves of the common people*'. He was thrown into a
common grave (cf. 2 Kings 23⁶).

26²⁴. '*Ahikam*'. The father of Gedaliah (see 39¹⁴). A man of
considerable influence (cf. 40⁵; 2 Kings 25²², 22¹²⁻¹⁷).

At this point we are given accounts of some important incidents
in the prophet's life. This group of narratives may have
been one of a number of sources from which the book was
compiled (26¹-29³²).

This first incident in the group occurs shortly after Jehoiakim
was put on the throne by the Egyptians (verse 1). The fact that
'*all the cities of Judah*' are represented in the congregation
may mean that the coronation festivities were still in progress
(verse 2). The attitude of the ordinary people is not very clear
(compare verses 8 and 16), but the priests and the prophets
were the accusers and it was some of the senior laymen who
defended Jeremiah (verses 17, 24). The Temple was the central
shrine of Judah and the prophet is accused, like Jesus and
Stephen centuries later, of blaspheming the holy place. His

only explanation for his action is that the Lord has sent him (verses 12, 15). But because the Lord has sent him he is prepared to stand by what he has said, even if this costs him his life (verse 14). Here we see again the amazing courage of Jeremiah; the Lord is fulfilling His promise (cf. 1^{17-18}), and giving him confidence. Although Jehoiakim has not been long in power, he has already been able to drag the prophet Uriah back from Egypt and have him put to death. Uriah's crime had been the uttering of a message similar to Jeremiah's, and now Uriah lay in the common grave. Death could easily have been the result for the man from Anathoth also, but he carried out his Lord's instructions.

What saved him was the timely recollection of the dealings of an earlier king with an earlier prophet (verses 18-19); also the intervention of powerful men who, though not prepared to obey a prophet's preaching, were prepared to respect it; but above all else, the faithfulness of the Lord to his obedient spokesman (cf. verse 5). One is reminded of Luther and his powerful protectors, and of Luther's saying, 'Even if I were to lose my body and my life on account of it, I cannot depart from the Word of God.'

This is one of the prophet's finest hours. Even when our neighbours become our enemies, love for them must not come to an end, but must show itself in a desire to restrain them from further sin (verse 15; cf. Acts 5^{29}).

27^1-28^{17}: Yokes of wood and yokes of iron

The time changes. It is now early in the reign of Zedekiah. The Lord tells the prophet to make yokes as a warning to some representatives of neighbouring nations who are visiting Judah.

Hananiah breaks the yoke that Jeremiah is wearing. But in due course the Lord tells Jeremiah that there is a yoke of iron now, in place of the yoke of wood, for His purpose is not changed. Hananiah is rebuked, and in less than two months he dies.

27^1. '*Jehoiakim*'. This is clearly wrong: see *RV*m. The incident belongs to a time early in the reign of Zedekiah, four years after the exile of Jehoiakim's son (Jehoiachin) to Babylon.

27². '*bands and bars*'. A wooden yoke with leather thongs, of the type fitted to cattle for ploughing or threshing.

27. '*Nebuchadnezzar*'. This is the incorrect form of the name given elsewhere as 'Nebuchadrezzar'.

27⁹. '*your prophets*'. Even the Gentile neighbours of Judah relied on such people. What makes men like Jeremiah different is that they serve the Lord.

27¹⁶. '*the vessels of the Lord's house*'. The Temple furnishings which had been taken to Babylon (cf. **52¹⁷⁻²³**, 2 Kings 24¹³, 25¹³⁻¹⁷).

27²². '*then will I . . . restore them*'. Cf. Ezra 1⁸.

This section probably incorporates material which was dictated to Baruch (cf. **27², ¹², ¹⁶, 28²**), and this may explain the editorial awkwardness in **28⁵⁻⁶**. Zedekiah had been put on the throne by Nebuchadrezzar in 598 BC but he is ready, four years later, to contemplate rebellion against Babylon. In fact no revolt took place at this stage, but it was postponed only until 589 BC. In **27³⁻¹¹** we have a good illustration of the responsibility of a '*prophet to the nations*' (cf. **1⁵, ¹⁰**). The Lord is in control and the dominance of Nebuchadrezzar is a sign, not of His powerlessness, but of His might. He can make even Babylon serve His purposes, and for as long as He pleases (**27⁶, ⁷**).

There are plenty of prophets among the Gentiles as well as in Judah, and most of the prophets in Judah are fit only to be classed with '*diviners*', '*soothsayers*' and '*sorcerers*'. Still, Jeremiah is prepared to accept the fact that Hananiah may be right, and indeed to hope that it is so (**28⁶**). But when, some time later (see *RSV* of **28¹²** and cf. **42⁷**), the word of the Lord comes, he is sure that Hananiah is seriously misleading God's people. The danger was all the more serious because there were so many people, both in Judah and in Babylon, who were counting on an early return of Jehoiachin from exile (cf. **22²⁴⁻³⁰, 27¹⁶**). It is only if nations work for Nebuchadrezzar that they will be allowed to work their own land. (There may be such a play on words in **27¹¹**.) Hananiah has to be told that the Lord has not '*sent*' him to prophesy, but He will '*send*' him—'*off the face of the earth*' (**28¹⁵⁻¹⁶**).

Judah may be a small and helpless nation, but her God is the supreme Lord of all the nations (27⁵). It is futile treacherous to ignore this: Nebuchadrezzar and his and descendants must rule until the Lord determines '*the time of his own land*' (27⁷). 'So dangerous a thing it is for ministers to teach people contrary to the revealed will of God' (Wesley's *Notes* on 28¹⁷).

Disaster is the only possible result of '*rebellion against the Lord*' (28¹⁶). To refuse the yoke that He offers (cf. Mt 11²⁸) is to refuse the only service in which we, or our nation, can find perfect freedom. The only authority that matters is derived from Him (cf. Jn 19¹⁰⁻¹¹). Even powerful rulers who serve other gods can be used by Him (cf. '*my servant*' in 27⁶ and see 43¹⁰, Isa 45¹). The only security lies in seeking first His kingdom. Even if our views on politics and international relationships may have to be more complex than those set forward in these chapters, the basic principles remain the same: God is the Lord of all history, of man and beast alike (cf. 27⁵⁻⁶), the only Ruler of all creation.

29¹⁻³²: The epistles of the prophet to the exiles

The time is a little earlier than chapters **27-8.** A year or two after Jehoiachin had been taken as a prisoner to Babylon, the prophet writes to the exiles there that it is God's will that they should settle down and lead normal lives.

29². '*Jeconiah*'. This is Jehoiachin; cf. **22²⁴⁻⁷.**
'*eunuchs*'. Perhaps better 'courtiers' or 'dignitaries'.

29³. '*Elasah the son of Shaphan*'. He may have been a brother of Ahikam; cf. **26²⁴.**

29⁸. '*neither hearken ye . . . dreamed*'. Read with *RSV*, 'do not listen to the dreams which they dream'.

29¹⁰. '*seventy years*'. See commentary on **25¹¹⁻¹².**

29¹⁵. '*prophets*'. They are named as '*Ahab*' and '*Zedekiah*' in verses 21-23. (Verse 21 should follow verse 15.) They were encouraging hopes among the exiles that Nebuchadrezzar would be overthrown.

29²¹. This should come directly after verse 15. The *LXX* does not include our verses 16-20 and they are probably an interpolation. Cf. **24⁸⁻¹⁰**.

'*Kolaiah*'. There is word-play on this name in verse 22, as it sounds like the Hebrew words for '*curse*' and '*roast*'.

29²⁴. Follow *RV*m.

29²⁶. '*mad*'. This is a reference to the frenzy and ecstasy which were still associated with the conventional types of prophesying.
'*shackles*'. Follow *RV*m.

29⁷ is remarkable as the only place in the OT to advocate prayer for Gentile enemies. One cannot help feeling that Jeremiah was open to such a word from the Lord, because he had learned already to pray in this way himself (cf. **18²⁰**). He is asking the exiles to pray for those who have taken them into exile, for those who have plundered the Temple, for those who hold captive the rightful King of Judah (cf. Mt 5⁴⁴⁻⁵, Lk 6²⁸).

Zedekiah would need to send representatives to his overlord in Babylon from time to time, and Jeremiah is able to send his letters by the hand of Elasah and Gemariah (verse 3). The exiles are not to be deluded by the '*dreams*' of mere '*diviners*' (verse 8). It is the Lord who has '*caused*' them '*to be carried away captive*' (verse 4), and His care over them now will be seen in the way He punishes Ahab and Zedekiah, men who are not only false prophets but who are also guilty of immorality (verses 21-3, cf. **23¹⁴**). It is not clear whether the message about Shemaiah (verses 24-9) was sent at this time, or even whether it was in written or oral form. Shemaiah has remonstrated with the Temple authorities for not punishing Jeremiah for his open opposition to the development of a 'resistance movement' among the exiles. Shemaiah's action is '*rebellion against the Lord*' (verse 32) and therefore he will have no descendant to see the eventual return of the exiles.

There are a number of indications here (and elsewhere in *Jer*) of the mood of the exiles in Babylon. Jehoiakim's folly had led to the deportation from Judah, not only of his widow

and son, but also of the cream of the population—the 'good
figs' of chapter **24**. Now they were settled on swampy, malarial
land, criss-crossed with canals that were no longer kept clean.
Far away from the hills of Judah, in the rank, tropical heat,
it must have been difficult not to start dreaming about an
early return to the places for which they were homesick.
Many of them must have been tempted to join in even the
most scatterbrained scheme in order to get back. They must
have been sorely tempted to rebel against the prophet's advice
to settle down—and as for praying for the welfare of the
Gentiles who had brought them to their plight! . . . It is not
surprising that some of them felt that Jeremiah was a raving
lunatic who should be clapped into the stocks and collar,
to bring him to his senses.

But the 'madman' was right. He had come a long and
painful way, and he knew in his very bones that being far
from the Lord was not a matter of geography, but an attitude
of life. The wonderful truth was beginning to be glimpsed that
God's people consists of those who know Him. They may be
handicapped by being sent away from the holy land for a time,
but they are not doomed. They may be 'displaced persons',
yet they are in the very position where the Lord can use them.
'*For I know the thoughts that I think toward you, saith the
Lord*'—to give you a latter end and hope (verse 11, see *RV*m).
What the Hebrew means is a future full of hope, a limitless
hope. The foundation of that hope is sure, because it is in the
'*thoughts*', in the mind of God. His intention for them is
'*peace*'—a peace that passes understanding, a perfect fulfilment
of His purpose of salvation. If only they will put their trust
in Him, there will surely come to their children the one
change of fortune that they desire above all others. For the
Lord will '*turn again*' their '*captivity*' (verse 14). In his advice
to '*build*' houses and '*plant gardens*', the prophet is exercising
his own calling '*to build, and to plant*' with great effect (verse
5, cf. **1**[10]); it is his work that the Lord uses to make possible
the resurrection of faith in the living God after the death of
His city and His temple (cf. Isa 57[15]). As C. H. Dodd has said,
'The post-exilic Jewish community is a fact of history simply
because the prophets had their vision of God' (*The Authority
of the Bible*. p. 242 of Fontana edition).

Here we have a prophet serving God by writing to people in

distant places and in difficult circumstances. He could well have written in an 'I told you this would happen' style, but he sends words of comfort. God is the One who always knows His own mind, and in His love He will certainly achieve all that He intends (verse 11). These firm promises of God are not intended to discourage us from prayer, but rather to encourage us (verse 12). Even a disaster as terrible as exile may be God's way of taking His children on towards the fulfilment of His good purpose for them. He is the God who comes to us, and He comes to us while we are yet sinners; we could never seek Him, unless first He had found us and we love Him because He first loved us. Wherever we are, whatever has happened, it is necessary—and possible—to seek the Lord. This involves recognizing that, precisely because He is our *Lord*, our seeking is futile unless it means accepting and obeying His will (*'with all your heart'*, verse 13). It is 'with those who love him' that 'in everything God works for good' (Rom 8²⁸ in *RSV*). And those who love Him set their hope, not chiefly on the temporal benefits He will provide for their children or children's children (as did the ancient Hebrew and as do some present-day Communists), but on His gift of eternal life, which can be received now, as a foretaste of things that surpass all our imagining.

30¹⁻²⁴: The future restoration of Israel and Judah

When discipline and punishment have done their work, the days will come when God will restore both Israel and Judah to their own land so that they may serve Him there.

30⁷. '*Jacob*'. The descendants of the people of Israel, the northern kingdom, who were taken into captivity in 721 BC (cf. verse 10).

30⁹. '*David*'. A descendant of the first King David.

30¹⁴. '*lovers*'. Former allies.

30¹⁸. '*I will turn again*'. Read, 'I will restore the fortunes of Jacob's tents'. The Hebrew text is full of confusions of *shebith* (captivity) with *shebuth* (fortune). Cf. 29¹⁴; Job 42¹⁰.
   '*the city . . . manner thereof*'. Jerusalem will be built again

on its own mound or 'tel' (see *RV*m), and the palace will be just where it was before it was destroyed.

30²¹. *'prince'*, *'ruler'*. Notice that a 'king' is not promised. But see verse 9.

30²³⁻²⁴. This is a repetition of **23¹⁹⁻²⁰** where the passage is in its right context. The *RV*m should be followed in verses 13 and 17.

The oracles collected in **30⁵-31²²** show again the prophet's concern for the exiles of the northern kingdom. There was a time during the reign of Josiah when Judah gained control for a brief period over Samaria and Galilee. Through all the troubles that have come since hopes rose high in those days, the prophet has never forgottten that God has purpose for those northerners in exile as well as for Judah. When they have learned that their 'sins are flagrant' and their 'guilt is great' (*RSV* of verse 14), there will come salvation. The process will be painful (verse 11), but in this way they can be restored to the position they were in after the first Exodus (verses 17, 20).

In these poems of hope for the northern kingdom we find that salvation involves (*a*) salvation from fear (verses 5-7), (*b*) salvation from slavery (verses 8-11), (*c*) salvation from powerlessness (verses 12-17), and (*d*) salvation from false religion (verse 21). It is salvation from these things into a society which is healthy because it is entirely guided by God, a happy royal priesthood of believers whose leaders rejoice in their access to the Lord (verses 17, 20, 21). These are the things that God does because His property is 'always to have mercy', because He is the righteous and gracious Saviour, and because His love never comes to an end. It is for these things that Israel is His 'servant' (verse 10; cf. Isa 43¹⁰⁻¹³, 44²¹⁻²). And if all this seems too good to be true when first we hear it, then it stands written *'in a book'* so that we can turn to it again and again (verse 2). Then, once a man has really heard *'I am with thee, saith the Lord, to save thee'*, it becomes true that *'none shall make him afraid'* (verses 10-11; cf. Ezek 34²²⁻⁸, 39²⁵⁻⁹). This comes about in the very place where it was said *'There is fear, and no peace'* (*RV*m of verse 5). In this way the Lord remains faithful to His covenant (verse 22); He goes on gathering the '*congregation*' of those to whom He has restored '*health*' (verses 17, 20).

31¹⁻⁶: Eternal love

A poem about God's love, the *chesed* that will not let Israel go.

31²⁻³. '*even Israel . . . of old unto me*'. As *RV*m indicates, there is some confusion here. Read, with some help from the *LXX*, 'when Israel longed for rest, the Lord appeared unto him from afar'.

31⁴. '*tabrets*'. The tambourines used by maidens on occasions of rejoicing (cf. Judges 21²¹).

31⁵. '*plant . . . and enjoy*'. The point is that newly planted vineyards do not become productive until they have had years of care. The picture is one of secure peace in '*Samaria*', the northern kingdom.

31⁶. '*Ephraim*'. Again the northern tribes. They will be at peace with Judah and will recognize '*Zion*' or Jerusalem again as the centre for the worship of the Lord. Cf. 4¹⁵. This of course is precisely what the Samaritans would not do (cf. Jn 4²⁰).

Verse 1 is the hinge between chapters **30** and **31**. We are still concerned with the northern tribes, with '*Israel*'. The poem in verses 2-6 is concerned with the '*everlasting love*' of God (verse 3), on which alone rests the hope of these northern Israelites. The word translated '*lovingkindness*' is *chesed* (verse 3). This important word stands for the covenant-love of God, a steadfast, faithful and invincible love, the love that 'will never come to an end' (*NEB* of 1 Cor 13⁸; cf. Hos 11⁸). See commentary above on 2², 3¹², and 9²⁴.

 There is nothing of the kill-joy about Jeremiah. In this lovely poem, which may come from the days when he was with Gedaliah at Mizpah near the '*mountains of Samaria*' and the '*hills of Ephraim*' (see **40⁶**), we see again his delight in the sights and sounds of a land at peace (verses 4-6, cf. 25¹⁰). Israel may be in the '*wilderness*' (verse 2), but, since God is the Redeemer from everlasting to everlasting, the wilderness

I

is still a place where '*grace*' may be '*found*'. Just as Israel learned to know the Lord there in Moses' day, so she can learn again, in order that once again she shall '*be built*' (verse 4. Cf. 2²⁻⁷).

The 'God we adore' is

> *Our faithful, unchangeable friend;*
> *Whose love is as great as His power,*
> *And neither knows measure nor end.* (*MHB* 69)

That is why we can 'trust Him for all that's to come'. This 'ceaseless, unexhausted love' (*MHB* 49) that comes to us in Jesus Christ will have its victory, in us and among all the nations. In Christ, Judah and Israel and every other separated group can be re-united. Christians are given a share in His 'ministry of reconciliation', until the day when the Saviour who loves us to the uttermost shall 'see light from the travail of His soul and be satisfied' (Isa 51¹¹ according to the Dead Sea Scroll and the *LXX*). The same love that may have to drive us into the wilderness is able to the end to '*draw*' (cf. verse 3) all men to Himself (Jn 12³²).

31⁷⁻²²: Comfort for Rachel's children

Though Rachel has been lamenting the trouble that has fallen upon her descendants, the Lord comforts her because, now that the Israelites are penitent, He will lead them back home, a great host of them, by the way they went.

31⁷. '*shout for the chief of the nations*'. This should be 'shout on the mountaintops' (cf. Isa 42¹¹).

31⁸. '*the north country*'. This is here synonymous with '*the uttermost parts of the earth*', the place of exile.

31⁹. '*a straight way*'. A level road that has been specially made up for their journey (cf. Isa 40³⁻⁴).

31¹². '*soul*'. Better, 'life'.
'*watered garden*'. Where there is water enough and to spare, in contrast with the surrounding desert (cf. Isa 58¹¹).

31¹⁵. '*Rachel*'. The 'mother' of the northern tribes.

'*Ramah*'. This follows the tradition that Rachel's sepulchre was here, and not at Bethlehem as others believed.

31¹⁷. '*hope for thy latter end*'. See commentary above on **29¹¹**.

31¹⁸. '*turn thou me . . .*'. Literally, 'make me return, so that I may return'.

31¹⁹. '*smote upon my thigh*'. A gesture of despair and sorrow (cf. Ezek 21¹²).

31²⁰. '*bowels*'. See commentary on **4¹⁹**. *RSV* paraphrases 'My heart yearns'.

31²². '*A woman shall encompass a man*'. This is a real puzzle. It possibly means that, at last, the Bride of the Lord will cling to Him. But this is only one of many desperate conjectures.

A possible link with Mizpah has been mentioned in the commentary above on verses 1-6 and here the reference to Ramah (verse 15) may be a clue linking this section with the same time in the prophet's life (cf. **40¹**). The fall of Jerusalem to the Chaldeans may have marked a watershed for Jeremiah, as well as for Judah, and it is not improbable that he was required to concentrate on reconstruction as long as Gedaliah was alive. His beautiful songs in the night arise from his faith that God's holy love is a fire that burns in order to refine and not merely to destroy (cf. verse 28). These poems may have influenced a later poet, the writer of Isaiah 40-55.

When the penitent, helpless '*remnant of Israel*' (verse 7) turns to God, He will attend to their '*supplications*' like a '*father*' (verse 9, cf. 3¹⁴, ¹⁹). Those who are now '*scattered*' (verse 10) will be gathered by the Good Shepherd, and because they hunger and thirst after righteousness they shall be filled. After the journey through the wilderness, they will revel in a garden abundantly supplied with water (verse 12, cf. Ps 23⁵). For God's discipline is the sign, not that His people are forgotten, but that they are remembered; those whom He loves He chastises, in order to bring them back into the good way (verse 20, cf. 1 Cor 11³², Heb 12⁶, Rev 3¹⁹). He alone can make repentance possible (verse 18) and bring in a new creation (verse 22). The way out of slavery to sin, and into the glorious liberty of the children of God (verse 20) is safe and well sign-posted (verse 21; cf. Isa 35[8]). It is the way that begins with God (verse 18) and that ends with Him (verse 25).

Our privilege is to be able to pray, 'Thou know'st the way to bring me back' (*MHB* 346), for the 'Shepherd of Israel' can be 'mine' also (*MHB* 457). God is the Saviour whose righteousness is shown in His being always on the side of the helpless (cf. verses 8-9, 11); He is the Shepherd who protects the helpless sheep (cf. Ps 23[4], Jn 10[14-15]). The same mighty 'arm' which rules 'for him' is used to 'gather the lambs' and 'gently to lead the ewes that are suckling them' (40[10-11]). This is still the work of 'the great shepherd of the sheep' who was brought again from the dead and is at the right hand of God. He knows the way to bring us back, and when we realize that this good Shepherd has laid down His life for the sheep, we cease to rebel like a young ox not broken in (verse 18). Instead we pray with the assurance that we shall be heard—'make me return, so that I may return' (verse 18. Notice the parallel with Augustine of Hippo's famous prayer, 'Give what Thou commandest, and command what Thou wilt'). It is all of God's grace: even our repentance is in His gift and is the response to His graciousness revealed in the way in which He has '*ransomed*' and '*redeemed*' us (verse 11, cf. Rom 2[4]). So there comes the moment when the time for chastisement is past, when the Father can fulfil His longing and make plain to His child the affection which governs His every action (cf. verses 9, 20). And for the child there comes the feeling that at last life is '*as a watered garden*' (verse 12, cf. **17**[5-8]; 1 Cor 3[6-8]), and the wonder that '*the Lord hath created a new thing in the earth*' (verse 22). In other words the prophet is speaking here of what the theologians describe as 'salvation by grace through faith'; the pattern of the course that has to be followed by Rachel's children has been followed by many a child of God. It begins with the Lord making Himself known to me as '*my God*' (verse 18), so that I become able to pray for repentance, so that I become contrite and ashamed of my days of rebellion and sinfulness (verse 19), so that I return by the '*way by which*' I went. It is a case of 'Right about, turn!', so that I come back to God from whom I went away.

This arrival back in God is the end of His causing me to turn to Him (verse 18).

These poems of hope were not fulfilled as far as the exiles from the northern kingdom were concerned. They became the 'lost' tribes. But the poems stand in Scripture because God's love is everlasting (verse 3) and His appeal is still to the lost (cf. Lk 15[11-24]). There is nothing on His side to make us remain exiles in the far country and the question is still '*How long?*' (verse 22).

31[23-6]: The restoration of Judah

The Lord shows the prophet in a dream that one day Judah will be restored, Jerusalem will be righteous, and all the land will be at peace.

31[23]. '*bring again*'. Better, 'restore them from'.

There is a very real contrast between things as they are and what God has prepared for those who love Him (cf. verse 26), and this hope refreshes and renews the prophet before he goes on with the work to which he is called among his contemporaries. Some commentators feel that these sentiments cannot be from Jeremiah, and suggest that verse 26 is a comment by an ironical early scribe who was of the same opinion. After this brief oracle on Judah the next section returns to a concern with Israel also (cf. verse 27).

31[27-40]: A new covenant and a new Jerusalem

The days are coming when the Lord will restore the fortunes of both Israel and Judah. He will deal with the sins of each of His people, and they shall each of them know Him, and obey Him from the heart. Against God's people the gates of Hades shall not prevail, and the new Jerusalem will be the truly holy city of the Lord.

31[38]. '*the tower of Hananel*'. At the north-east corner.
'*the gate of the corner*'. At the north-west.

31[39]. '*Gareb*', '*Goah*'. These have not been identified, but may be points marking the south-west and south-east corners.

31⁴⁰. '*valley of the dead bodies, and of the ashes*'. The valley of Hinnom (cf. **7³¹, 32³⁵**).

In the end, God's reconstruction will take place. He will be 'wakeful' then '*to build, and to plant*', as He has been '*to destroy and to overthrow*' (cf. verse 28 which is clearly linked with **1¹⁰, ¹²**). When that time comes, God will free men from the burden of their predecessors' wrongdoing and leave them with responsibility for their own behaviour only (verses 29-30). In place of the old covenant, written on the tablets of stone, there will be a new covenant, inscribed on the hearts of each one of God's people, in the handwriting of their forgiving Lord (verses 31-4).

Jeremiah is obsessed with the problem of why God's people continually fail to profit, in the way they ought to do, from the covenant which the Lord granted to them at Sinai (see **6¹⁶⁻²¹, 7⁵⁻¹⁰, ²²⁻³, 26⁴⁻⁶**). Even as recently as the time of Josiah's 'Reformation' they had solemnly reaffirmed their loyalty to the Lord, yet ever since they had clearly been ignoring or even despising His instruction. What is needed is a new '*heart*', a miracle whereby there is brought into being a '*house of Israel*' (verse 33), whose characteristic is the 'knowledge' of God, and they are to be '*a nation before*' Him '*for ever*' (verse 36). So the purpose of God will be fulfilled in a nation reconciled to Him, wherein all the Lord's people are prophets (verses 35-7; cf. **9²⁴**). Then it will be true that in the holy city the tabernacle of God is with men (cf. Rev 21¹⁻⁵), and even Gehenna '*shall be holy unto the Lord*' (verse 30; cf. **7³¹**).

The '*covenant*' is not a bargain or contract between equals: it is something that *the Lord* makes. It is a bond conferred by the Stronger on the weak (cf. **34⁸⁻¹⁰**). It is a sign of God's saving grace, and should reasonably meet with the response of humble, grateful trust and obedience. Thus, pride, unbelief, ingratitude or disobedience among God's people are always a flouting of the covenant. The basis of the new covenant is still the will of the Lord, but this covenant touches the '*heart*' (verse 33). It grips and changes the will, the very self, of each one who is brought within it.

This concept of covenant is so fundamental in Scripture that the two parts of our Bible are known as the books of the Old Covenant and the books of the New Covenant—the word 'testament' being an old translation of 'covenant' (see 2 Cor 3[6, 14]). One valuable clue to the understanding of 'covenant' is that it is like a Hebrew marriage (cf. verse 32 and *Hosea passim*). In OT times a bridegroom had to pay a bride-price. Usually the bride had no choice in the matter and, once married, her husband was her lord and master whom she could never divorce. So God's people is called to be His Bride, His peculiar possession, His royal treasure. He will never swerve in His loyalty to her, and she will find Him worthy of absolute trust. She has the privilege of worshipping and serving Him in gratitude; this is the only reasonable response to her divine Husband's constant love, so completely generous, and so completely unmerited.

The oracles in verses 27-30 and 38-40 may have become attached to verses 31-37 chiefly because they open with the words '*Behold, the days come, saith the Lord*' (see verses 27, 38, 31). Still it is useful to have these two other pictures of what a prophet believed would come on that eagerly longed for 'New Age Day' which would mark the beginning, not merely of a new year, but of a New Age. Verses 27-30 remind us that one of the things that has to be settled is the relationship between the individual and the community, and verses 38-40 promise a city that is '*built to the Lord*' (verse 38), where everything is transformed, even Gehenna, because it is '*holy unto the Lord*' (verse 40). The writer of *Revelation* knew that this city —'new Jerusalem'—could only come down out of heaven from God (Rev 2[12], 21[2, 5, 10]).

The passage on the '*new covenant*' (verses 31-4) has come to have so many overtones and harmonies for the preacher of the gospel that it is important, in the first instance, to listen to what the prophet is saying. We must beware of finding here a sort of Magna Carta of individualism. The NT is in a sense more individualist than the prophet could be, because it recognizes that those who belong to God's family must be 'born again'. It is only when each of us is made right with God that we come to be conscious participants in the fellowship of those that believe. Jeremiah cannot see *how* each man can come to know the Lord for himself, but he believes that the Lord will bring this about in His own way. The essence of the covenant is still '*I will be their God, and they shall be my people*' (verse 33; cf. Deut 4[20], 29[13]), but it applies to a far bigger group than the prophet envisaged when he spoke of the *'house of Israel'* and the *'house of Judah'* (verse 31). Jeremiah is concerned with a whole people that has turned its back on God and betrayed its heritage: Jesus comes and shows that He is prepared to deal with each lost sheep, as well as with the whole flock, for that is God's way of making Himself known to each one of us, *'from the least unto the greatest'*.

The OT is not nearly so ignorant as we are sometimes asked to believe of the fact that the Lord who is related to His people is also related to individuals among them. One has only to recall persons such as Moses, the Judges, Samuel, Elijah, and David; and certainly Jeremiah knew this truth in his own experience. It may be that the exiles in Babylon were using the old idea, that God visits the sins of the forefathers on their descendants, to shield themselves against the true significance of the disaster that had come upon them. But the prophet has no hesitation about reminding them that each of them is accountable to God (verse 30; cf. Ezek 14[13-14], 18[1-32], Deut 24[16]), even if the rule of *'every one shall die for his own iniquity'* can become fully effective only *'in those days'* in the happy future. Perhaps the prophet was not quite so unsound about recognizing that communalism can devour personality, as we may have been told. And most certainly he can give us a salutary reminder that individualism can ruin community. In the community of those who *'know the Lord'*, every one is a *'brother'* since we have a common Father; every one is a 'neighbour' whom the Lord has appointed as His collector of the debt we owe to Him (verse 34). The last word about the relationship of the individual to society has not been said, and will not be said in our time, but at least the 'covenant' points to a solution, because it brings about a situation where both community and individual are subject to a common Lord.

John Wesley insisted that it is unscriptural to hanker after anything in the category of 'solitary religion' (cf. Jn 13[35], 1 Jn 4[7, 20-1]). Once God adopts us, we find ourselves in a family where we cannot have Him without having also the brothers and sisters He has already adopted, and those He will adopt in the future. An essential part of His gift of salvation is that now we are bound together in the bundle of life with the rest of His people, so that it is only 'in company with' them that we can reach 'perfection' (cf. Heb 11[40], *NEB*). Even when all the Lord's people are prophets, when each of us belongs to

God's fellowship class (verse 34; cf. **23**[18]), we remain a *'people'*. Indeed we become more a people than ever since we are the congregation of Christ, against which even the powers of death cannot prevail. Jesus binds Himself to His Church of the new covenant and we therefore believe in the resurrection of the body—we believe that each of us is saved as a member of the community which is His Body.

There are four key words in verses 31-34: (*a*) *'covenant'*, (*b*) *'heart'*, (*c*) *'know'* and (*d*) *'forgive'*. The *'covenant'* is God's work. He takes the initiative again. Jeremiah who knows that he was himself chosen before he was born (**1**[5]) has had it revealed to him that the Lord is prepared to begin again (cf. Isa 54[8], Hos 2[18-20]. The whole passage Hos 2[14-23] is most important in connection with the teaching of *Jer*). This is not something that can be taken for granted; it has been *made known* to the prophet, in a whisper that he can shout from the housetops (Mt 10[27], *NEB*). This is the point of the repetition of *'saith the Lord'*, four times in four verses. This may seem to be stylistically clumsy, but it indicates a solemn insistence on something that the Lord has revealed to his prophet. This is Jeremiah's way of saying, 'Verily, verily, the Lord says . . .'. The time has not yet come when God speaks directly to each of His people (cf. Deut 18[15-22]), but He reveals His secret to his prophet (cf. **23**[18], Amos 3[7]). Notice also the repetition *'I will make'*, *'I will put'*, I will *'write'*, *'I will be'*, *'I will forgive'* and I will not *'remember'*. All is of God. Salvation is by grace, and not by natural right. It rests on a covenant made by One who is the 'lord over' us (see *RV*m of verse 32). He pays the bride-price in the outpouring of the life of His Son. How can we refuse to accept the new relationship He offers, and be blind to the logical response of spending our lives in giving Him thanks?

This leads us on to the problem of the *'heart'* (verse 33, cf. Hos 2[14] in *RV*m). We have noticed the prophet's preoccupation with the need to set things right in men's *'inward parts'*. This is where he found the trouble lay in himself, and he knew that something revolutionary was needed, something that human beings can never do for themselves. Sin is engraven on the heart (**17**[1]) but *'the days come'* when the Lord's rule will be written there instead. The time is coming when His will shall be written into the lives of His people and they will serve Him from the *'heart'*. (See 3[17], 4[4, 14], 5[23], 7[24], 9[14, 25-6], **11**[8],

13^{10}, 16^{12}, 17^9, 18^{12}, 23^{17}; cf. Ezek 11^{19}, 18^{31}, 36^{26}, Jn 3^7.) This is the supreme problem in life: how is the '*heart*' of each of us to be radically changed? This does not mean that we are to have no interest in politics or economics or international affairs, any more than it meant that Jeremiah had no such interest. But it does mean that we are to keep a proper sense of proportion about these things. The centre of the problem is the '*heart*'. How it was to be dealt with, the prophet did not know, but his faith was that God would act effectively '*after those days*'.

This faith was reasonable, since Jeremiah believed that the whole purpose of the religious, political, legal and social rules which had developed among God's people was to lead them to the '*knowledge*' of God. This '*knowledge*' is a word so rich in its implications that it is almost impossible to translate. '*Knowledge*' here stands for a whole relationship which is so intimate that even the deepest intimacy between man and wife is but a reflection of it (cf. Gen 4^1). When the Lord marries Himself to His people in a permanently binding relationship, He makes Himself 'known' to them and they enter upon a new way of life. This is their 'knowing' of Him, a personal relationship of choice and response, of giving and receiving, of caring and being cared for. This union of Lord and Bride is a *covenant* (cf. Ezek 16^{59-62}), and the Bride's 'knowing' is her enjoyment of, and acknowledgement of, His care. Such 'knowledge' is in fact 'faith'—a steadfast reliance on God, and obedience to Him, which is seen in all our dealings with our fellow men. (See Hos 2^{19-20}; cf. 2^2, 24^7, 4^{22}, 5^4, 8^7, $9^{3,\,6,\,23-4}$, Hos $4^{1,\,6}$, 5^4, 6^6, Isa 43^{1-2}, and *RSV* of 63^9; Ps 14, 53 and 139).

This insight is developed in the NT. Where God makes Himself known, there comes into existence a Servant of the Lord, a people that is for Him, and that acts gratefully because of its knowledge. Knowledge is a way of life, a gift of God; it is living as people who have received His grace. It does not concern just a part of us, such as our mind or our emotions; it involves our whole being. It is a being brought 'near' to God (Eph 2^{13}) and its opposite is not so much ignorance as separation, a being 'without God' (cf. Eph 4^{18}) which is death (see Mt 25^{12}). It is essentially a being known by God in the first instance: we know Him only because He first knows us, and therefore this kind of knowledge is the last thing to lead us to become 'puffed up' (1 Cor 8¹, 13⁴; cf. Gal 4⁹, 1 Cor 13¹²). Jeremiah could not see how his prophecy was to be fulfilled, whereas we can. The key passages are Matthew 11²⁷⁻³⁰ and John 10¹⁴ (cf. Jn 10²⁷, 17³, ²⁵⁻⁶, 1 Cor 8¹⁻³, Eph 3¹⁹, Phil 3⁸⁻¹¹).

Still this knowledge is not perfect. '*The days come*' when we shall at last attain, and our knowledge will be whole, like God's knowledge of us (cf. Eph 4¹³, 1 Cor 13¹²).

Jeremiah could not see clearly, or expect his contemporaries to see clearly, how it would come about that God would deal with the '*heart*' and make men to '*know*' Him in a New Age. What they could see was like baffling reflections in a mirror. This applies perhaps even more to their conception of how the Lord would '*forgive*' (verse 34). The writer to the Hebrews recognizes that the new covenant is new, not because the Lord's purpose has in any way changed, but because it is based on 'better promises' (Heb 8⁶), and will therefore lead to a community of those who are responding spontaneously to His purpose. The better promises are (*a*) that God's claims will be written on our heart, so that 'Thy will be done' is a part of our very being, (*b*) that we all shall '*know*' the Lord and (*c*) that we shall be forgiven, the burden of our guilt will be removed, so that all life becomes a thanksgiving for such deliverance. It is doubtful whether the prophet realized how wonderful this third promise, 'the most impossible of all', was to prove. This promise pointed, as we are allowed to know in our time, to the Last Supper and Calvary, to the sealing of the covenant with the blood of the only-begotten Son of God. This is in fact how it can happen that God's forgiveness marks the beginning of a new life with Himself for each member that He calls into the community of His New Israel (cf. Heb 8⁶⁻¹³, 9¹⁵, 10¹⁷⁻¹⁸). Jeremiah had a foretaste of the new day when 'grace gives what it demands' (Pascal); he himself could feel the 'finger of God' (Ex 31¹⁸) writing, not on 'tables of stone' but on his own personality. But when it came to forgiveness he had heard not the faintest echo of that 'song which even angels can never, never sing' because 'they know not Christ as Saviour' (*MHB* 839). Jesus is the one who gives 'the new covenant' in His own blood (see 1 Cor 11²⁵, Mk 14²⁴).

The prophet knew that a miracle was needed and believed

that it would happen, but when or how he could not see (cf. **23**⁷⁻⁸). Now it has happened (see Eph 2¹¹⁻²⁰, 2 Cor 3⁶, Heb 1⁴, 7²², 12²⁴). We know of a surety that the God of creation and the God of grace are one and the same (verses 35-7; cf. Isa 54⁵); the Creator of the ends of the earth and of the universe comes to us in Jesus Christ. In the Lord's Supper we 'remember' the covenant that He has made with us and His Church as the result of the Exodus (the word translated 'decease' in Lk 9³¹) that He accomplished from sin and from death. It is good for us to know that now every '*heart*' can be made firm and stable on the solid, unshakeable foundation of His grace (cf. Heb 13⁹). By faith we see the glory of God in the face of Jesus Christ and rejoice to be known of Him and to '*know*' Him; we have the privilege of receiving the command, 'When ye pray say, Our Father'. Once the prophet hoped for the day when Israel would consist of people who 'know' the Lord; now the good news is that those who '*know*' the Lord, whether they be Jew or Gentile, are the Israel of God. So it is true that

> *Blest are the pure in heart* . . .
> *The secret of the Lord is theirs.*   (*MHB* 950)

But it is also true that still '*the days come*' (verse 31) and then 'they shall see their God'. We 'remember' the 'new covenant' until the Lord comes, because when He comes the promise made to Jeremiah will have its perfect fulfilment in His Kingdom, where every knee shall bow, and every tongue confess that He is Lord. *Behold, the days come.*

32¹⁻⁴⁴: The field at Anathoth

During the siege of Jerusalem in 587 B C, the prophet's cousin offers to sell his land at Anathoth, as the Lord had predicted. Although he is in prison, Jeremiah buys the land and takes great care to have the deeds preserved.

32¹. '*the tenth year of Zedekiah*'. The year in which the city fell (cf. **52**⁵⁻⁷, 2 Kings 25¹⁻²).

32². '*shut up*'. See **37**²¹, **38**²⁸ for this imprisonment.

32⁷. '*the right of redemption is thine*'. The prophet is the 'redeemer' or *go'el*, whose right and duty it is to defend the interests of the family (cf. Lev 25²⁵). The purpose of the rule was to keep land in the same family.

32⁹. '*weighed*'. Payments were made by weight of metal.
'*seventeen shekels*'. The 'shekel' is a weight, not a coin. The amount would be about seven ounces of silver.

32¹⁰. '*subscribed*'. Or 'signed'—he wrote his name at the bottom. The whole transaction was carried out carefully in proper legal form, '*according to the law and custom*' (verse 11).

32¹¹. '*open*'. The original was '*sealed*', but the duplicate attached to it was open for easy reference. The sealed original would be consulted only if there was reason to believe that the open duplicate had been tampered with.

32¹². '*Baruch*'. This is the first mention in the book of the prophet's amanuensis.

32¹⁴. '*an earthen vessel*'. Documents were preserved in pottery jars. Cf. the 'Dead Sea Scrolls'.

32²⁴. '*mounts*'. Better, 'siege-mounds', built by the Chaldeans.

32²⁹. '*roofs*'. Cf. **19¹³**.

32³⁵. '*Molech*'. Cf. **7³¹**, 2 Kings 23¹⁰. It was to Melek that children were sacrificed.

(**19⁵** is mistaken in referring to '*burnt offerings unto Baal*' and this is omitted in the *LXX*.) '*Molech*' is the way a Hebrew pronounced 'Melek' when he wished to be insulting to the pagan god; for the vowels of Melek he substituted the vowels of *bosheth* ('shameful thing', cf. **11¹³**, **3²⁴**). See also *TWB*, 97-8.

32⁴⁴. '*I will cause their captivity to return*'. Better, 'I will restore their fortunes' (see commentary on **30¹⁸**).

The siege began in '*the ninth year of Zedekiah*' (**39¹**). The prophet has been in the miry '*dungeon*' and has been rescued. He is now under restraint in the palace courtyard (verse 2; cf. 38[6, 13, 28]). A man without wife or child, a miserable prisoner who may soon be done to death, he buys a plot of land that he may never see, a field that may already be in the hands of the invader. He does this as a *sign*. It is done where everyone can see, '*before all the Jews*' (verse 12), so that they may know that the same love which is now about to destroy is determined also '*to build and to plant*'. It is a dramatic sign of Jeremiah's confidence in the purpose of the Lord to give to His people, in the days beyond the certain and terrible disaster that is shortly to happen, a future filled with hope. Like Abraham centuries before at Machpelah (Gen 23[3-20]), the prophet is required to back his trust in the faithfulness of God with hard cash (verse 9). The incident may mark an important turning-point in the thinking of Jeremiah, the point when (in doing his duty by his family, even though it seemed ridiculous), he was allowed to glimpse the miracle of renewal which lay far ahead in God's purpose for Judah. From this point onwards it becomes more likely that he will be able to write the poems of chapter **31**.

Verses 16-44 seem to belong to a period some considerable time '*after*' he '*delivered the deed of purchase unto Baruch*'. There are signs that the material that comes from the prophet has been expanded by later disciples of Jeremiah who wished to pack into this section as much teaching as possible (cf. Neh 9[6-38]).

Here we have a significant indication that a prophet had no extraordinary means of deciding what is and what is not a '*word of the Lord*'. Jeremiah was in prison because he had set off, while the siege was temporarily lifted, to go to Anathoth '*to receive his portion there*' (37[12]). Whether this attempted visit was connected with Hanamel's field we do not know. But the prophet has a presentiment, which he suspects may be a '*word of the Lord*', that his cousin will be coming to ask him to buy the land. It was when Hanamel came that the prophet '*knew*' (verse 8) that his suspicions had been correct. The Lord has brought Hanamel to him just as surely as the Lord once led him to see the almond rod and the boiling caldron, and the potter's clay (1[11-16], 18[1-6]). Because it is a '*word of the Lord*', it has to be obeyed, and so, '*I bought the field*'. It is most unlikely that Jeremiah ever had any use of the field.

We do not know whether he ever set eyes on it, before he was dragged off to Egypt. He may have been tempted to think that once again the Lord had 'deceived' him, and when that happens the time comes for him to say, '*I prayed*' (verse 16). He has to be assured again that nothing is too 'wonderful' for the Lord (this is the meaning of the word translated '*hard*' in verse 27; cf. Isa 9⁶, 28²⁹, 29¹⁴). See *RV*m of verse 17.

Notice the careful construction of the prayer in verses 17-25. It begins with adoration of the almighty and merciful Creator of all things, whose care is over all His creatures so that each one receives what he needs (verses 17-19). He is the Saviour, the Redeemer of His people (verses 20-2). Then comes confession and contrition, and acceptance of His righteous judgement (verses 23-4). Only then comes the petition of the prophet (verse 25). The answer, when it comes, is a confirmation of the message that the prophet has been required to proclaim from the outset. God must hurl His unrepentant people from their land, but '*the days come*' (cf. 31³¹) when He will change their '*heart*' (verse 39) and make '*an everlasting covenant with them*' (verse 40) that '*they shall be my people, and I will be their God*' (verse 38). This is an anticipation of the teaching that is set out in 31²⁷⁻³⁷, the faith that all that the Lord does is '*for the good of them, and of their children after them*' (verse 39), even though this may not be evident to all men until '*the days come*'.

Faith has always led to actions that are costly and that may look ridiculous in the eyes of the world (cf. Heb 11¹-12²). This incident is a good illustration of the statement that 'Faith gives assurance to our hopes, and makes us certain of realities we do not see' (Heb 11¹, *NEB*). Happy is the man who lives in the faith that his future, and the future of the universe, belong to the God and Father of our Lord Jesus Christ; this is the faith that is ready for adventure, the faith that takes risks without knowing what the consequences may be. It may mean sacrificing 'our career' to what we believe to be the will of God, like Dr Albert Schweitzer. It may mean trying to witness as a Christian community inside an apparently impregnable Communist state. It may mean missionary work without 'results', continuing for decade after decade among Moslems. But we have an advantage which Jeremiah could not know— see Hebrews 12¹⁻³.

33¹⁻²⁶: God will restore

Jeremiah is a prisoner, but the Lord tells Him that His will
for His people cannot be finally defeated. What is now a
desolation shall again be the centre for worship. He will
cleanse Jerusalem. She will be named 'The Lord is our
righteousness', and He will make her glorious in the eyes of
the nations.

33¹. '*the second time*'. This is intended to link with **32¹⁻²**.

33². '*that doeth it*'. Better, 'who made the earth'.

33³. '*difficult*'. Better, 'hidden'; see *RV*m.

33⁴. '*broken down*'. Apparently some property near the city
wall had to be demolished to make it easier for the besieged
to try to deal with the Chaldean siege-mounds (cf. '*against the
mounts*'). See Isaiah 22⁹⁻¹⁰.

33⁵. The Hebrew is difficult. Read, 'the Chaldeans come to
fight and fill them with the bodies of men . . .'

33¹³. '*him that telleth*'. Sheep were counted as they went in or
out of the fold by being made to '*pass under the hand*' of the
shepherd.

33²⁴. '*two families*'. Israel and Judah.

33²⁶. Cf. **32⁴⁴** and commentary on **30¹⁸**.

Verses 14-26, which are not in the *LXX*, are probably an
editorial addition (cf. **32¹⁶⁻⁴⁴**). The breaking down of houses to
help the defenders during the siege may have reminded the
prophet of his own calling '*to break down, and to destroy
and to overthrow*' and also '*to build, and to plant*' (**1¹⁰**). After
the destruction that has already begun, and that must continue
till its dreadful end, the Lord will reverse the desolation and
Jerusalem will be again '*a name of joy*' (verse 9; cf. **31³⁸⁻⁴⁰**).
On the foundation of God's forgiveness (verse 8; cf. **31³⁴**)
they will have life in '*abundance*' (verse 6). The God whose
'*ordinances of heaven and earth*' cannot be broken (verse 25;

cf. 31³⁵⁻⁶) is the Lord who gives His people righteousness (verses 15-16; cf. Isa 45²⁴). Verses 15-16 are repeated from 23⁵⁻⁶, but now it is Jerusalem, and not the king, that is called *'The Lord is our righteousness'*.

'Righteousness' is God's activity, and our righteousness as His people can only come because He chooses to forgive the repentant and to cleanse them from 'all the guilt of their sin and rebellion' against Himself (verse 8 in *RSV*). There are three aspects here of the evil that separates us from God: (*a*) *'iniquity'* which stands for a warping or twisting; (*b*) *'sin'* which is missing the mark; (*c*) *'transgression'* (the Hebrew means literally 'rebellion') which is the wilful refusal to do what God requires. God's cleansing and pardon deal with the warping and twisting of our human nature, with all our sin and rebelliousness, and bring us instead *'health'*, *'peace'* and *'truth'* (verse 6).

> *Thy name salvation is . . .*
> *Thy name is life and health and peace*
> *And everlasting love.*   (*MHB* 718)

Notice also that *'peace'* is created and sustained by the righteous activity of God: it can only exist in conjunction with His righteousness and truth (verses 8-14; cf. Isa 54¹⁴, 60¹⁷, Zech 8¹⁶, ¹⁹, Ps 85⁹⁻¹⁰).

34¹⁻⁷: Zedekiah's future

Jerusalem must fall, but the king is told that, if he surrenders, he will go into honourable captivity in Babylon, and will die there in peace.

34²⁻⁵. Cf. 32⁴⁻⁵.

34⁵. *'a burning'*. Spices were burned at royal funerals. Notice references in *RV*m.

'Ah lord'. See commentary on 22¹⁸.

34⁷. *'Lachish'*, *'Azekah'*. These two fortresses (*'fenced cities'*) were on the border between Judah and Philistia. It is interesting to know that potsherds found in the ashes of Lachish in 1935 have letters written on them which reveal the confusion

K

of these days at the end of Zedekiah's reign. One of the letters refers to not being able to 'see the signals of Azekah'.

This message seems to date from the time just before Nebuchadrezzar laid siege to Jerusalem. The king did not accept the advice that the prophet took to him, and, instead of dying a natural death in Babylon and being buried with full royal honours, he was blinded at Riblah and ended his days in prison (52¹¹; cf. Ezek 12¹³).

34⁸⁻²²: A breach of faith

During the early part of the siege of Jerusalem, all Hebrew slaves were set free. But when the enemy withdrew, this act of emancipation was cancelled. Therefore the Lord is going to bring back the enemy and He will withdraw from the slave-owners their freedom to escape from the horror of defeat.

34¹⁰. '*princes*'. The leading officials.

34¹⁷. Follow *RV*m.

34¹⁸. '*when they cut the calf*'. Cf. Gen 15⁹⁻¹⁵. The *RSV* may be misleading at this point. It is not a question of calling down on themselves the end inflicted on the calf, but of both parties to the covenant being taken into the life of the victim.

34²¹. '*gone up*'. The besiegers had withdrawn from Jerusalem (cf. 37⁵).

There is a rather longwinded editorial introduction (verses 8-11; cf. verses 21-2, 37⁵⁻¹⁰). During the siege Zedekiah reminded his subjects of one of their obligations under the Mosaic law, which they had solemnly reaffirmed in the time of Josiah. Those who had become a people by being delivered out of bondage were required to have a special attitude to slavery among themselves (cf. Mt 6¹²). So the masters solemnly agreed before God in His Temple to obey Him (verse 15); but when the siege was lifted so that the Chaldeans could deal with the threat from an Egyptian army, these people broke faith. Not only did they break a promise made to their slaves and their king, but they went back on the agreement to do what was right in the Lord's eyes. In breaking the covenant made with their fellows, they broke the covenant that the Lord has made with His people (verse 18). God will bring back the enemy and the fate of these covenant-breakers will be terrible (verse 20).

Promises made to our fellow-men, even in times of desperation, are promises made to God. This applies to the promises that nations make to each other, to promises that trade unions and employers make to each other, as well as to the promises that one person may make to another. How pleased God is when we keep our agreements, even belatedly (notice '*now*' in verse 15); and how great is our danger when we offend Him by not keeping them. When we are in real trouble, most of us are very ready to make spoken or unspoken vows to God, and sometimes, when the trouble lifts, we find it convenient to forget. These promises are to be kept, or one day we may find God keeping His promises to deal with covenant-breakers. There is here, too, the truth that God's dealing with us ought to be reflected in the way we deal with other people (cf. Mt 6⁹⁻¹⁵, Lk 6³⁷⁻⁸). It is a mockery to God to break a solemn oath, and God is not mocked.

35¹⁻¹⁹: The steadfast Rechabites

The Rechabites are faithful to the commands of an ancestor, yet God's people are persistently unfaithful to the commands of their Lord.

35². '*house*'. The 'clan' of the Rechabites.

35⁶. '*father*'. In the sense of 'founder', the distant ancestor of the clan.

35¹¹. '*Syrians*'. These were the Aramean allies of Nebuchadrezzar in the invasion of Judah in 602 B C. Cf. 2 Kings 24¹⁻².

The Rechabite clan were descended from the Jonadab who supported Jehu in his attack on the worship of the baal of Tyre (cf. 2 Kings 10¹⁵⁻²⁸). The customs he gave to his clan (verses 6-7) were intended to revive the nomadic way of life, to make them independent of settled agriculture which had been seen to lead to a recognition of the pagan gods of fertility. Although force of circumstances had driven the Rechabite clan into the fortress of Jerusalem, they did not allow this to provide an excuse for infidelity to their traditions (verse 11). The incident is, of course, some fifteen years earlier than chapter 34 (cf. 25[1], 36[1]).

Jeremiah is not commending the Rechabites for being staunch teetotallers; he is not expressing his judgement on the rightness or the wrongness of the tradition to which they adhere: the whole point is their *faithfulness*. If they hold firmly to a family tradition that goes back over two centuries, how much more should God's people keep to the way He has prescribed for them (cf. Mt 5[20])! Again the prophet has provided a visual and dramatic aid to emphasize the Lord's plea, 'Turn and live' (cf. verse 15), but Judah will not listen.

It is far easier to stick to the standards of our home, our school, our neighbourhood, our profession, our workmates etc. than to persevere in the way of the Lord. Sometimes these traditions are a help, sometimes an obstacle, and sooner or later we have to learn to go beyond them or even to defy them. It is difficult to be the odd man out, to stand firm against wrong attitudes that are generally reckoned to be right because they have become fashionable. But we have only one Judge, and it is only in His service that there is perfect freedom. The finest thing that can happen to those who have learned to be faithful in a small thing, in being loyal to a tradition, is that God shall bring them to '*stand before*' Himself as His servants, so that they may be faithful to Him (cf. verse 19, **15[19]**; Mt 5[20], 25[21], Lk 16[10]). The most wonderful form of steadfastness is that which is founded on the faithfulness, the steadfast love, of God.

A preacher living in an area where Moslems, Christians and animists are living side by side has sometimes to point out that the Moslems are being more faithful to their traditions (e.g. regular prayer and abstinence from alcoholic drink) than the Christians are in their following of Jesus Christ. This accounts to some extent for the fact that more animists are becoming Moslems than are becoming Christian. The point at issue is not whether Islam is better than Christianity, but whether Moslems are more *faithful* than Christians in the eyes of their neighbours.

36¹⁻³²: The burning of a scroll

In December 604 B C, the Lord instructs the prophet to dictate
the messages that had come to him up to that time. For,
although he was under arrest, the people might be persuaded
to listen to a reading of his message. The prophecies are written
out by Baruch. The king listens to a reading of the messages,
but as the reader comes to the end of each section, Jehoiakim
cuts it from the scroll and throws it into the fire, even though
some of his counsellors try to dissuade him. The king orders
the capture of both the prophet and Baruch. But the Lord
hides them and instructs Jeremiah to dictate an even fuller
record, this time including a message about the end of Jehoiakim.

36². '*a roll of a book*'. A large papyrus scroll.

36⁵. '*I am shut up*'. He is not in prison, but he is forbidden
access to the Temple. He was perhaps under 'house arrest'.
See *RV*m. Cf. **33¹**.

36⁶. '*the fast day*'. Cf. verse 9. It may have been connected with
a drought, or with the recognition that there was danger from
the rising power of Chaldea (cf. **46²**).

36¹². '*the scribe's chamber*'. Probably the king's secretary's
room (cf. **37¹⁵**).
  '*the princes*'. The officials, the leading men.

36²². '*the ninth month*'. Of a year beginning in the spring, i.e.
November-December. The king is in his winter quarters and
the room is heated by a '*brasier*'.

36²³. '*leaves*'. Each time the reader came to the end of three or
four 'columns' (*RV*m), the king slashed off that section with a
'*penknife*', the type of knife used by scribes to sharpen their
reed pens.

36²⁴. '*rent their garments*'. Josiah had torn his robes at the
reading of the book found in the Temple. See 2 Kings 22¹¹.

36²⁶. '*the king's son*'. Probably not a member of the royal family
but a police official; cf. **38⁶**, 1 Kings 22²⁶⁻⁷.

The time is shortly after the Chaldeans had driven back the Egyptians from Carchemish (verses 1, 9; cf. 46²). The prophet is no longer in any doubt about the identity of the foe from the '*north*'. There is no time to lose in persuading his people to repent. Jeremiah is 'restrained' (*RV*m of verse 5), perhaps as a result of the events recorded in chapter 26 or 20¹⁻³ (cf. 26²⁴). He has to resort to an amanuensis. Notice that prophecies are things to be *spoken* to one's contemporaries; they are written only in exceptional circumstances. The time chosen for the reading again shows the Lord's desire that everyone should have the chance of hearing the warning. The officials are astonished (verse 16), and have to be assured that there is no mystery about the origin of this scroll such as there had been about the one discovered in Josiah's time (see 2 Kings 22⁸⁻¹¹). Perhaps remembering the fate of Uriah (see 26²⁰⁻³), they advise Baruch and the prophet to hide (verse 19). Jehoiakim is contemptuous of the prophecy, as they had anticipated. He regards the prophet as a disloyal supporter of the upstart Chaldeans and intends to have him liquidated. But God has other plans (verse 26); His word is not bound. Though His warnings are treated with scorn, or disregarded, they still stand (verses 30-31; cf. 22¹⁸⁻¹⁹). Jehoiakim in fact died and had, so far as we know, a normal funeral. His son sat on the throne, though only for a hundred days, before he was taken off to Babylon, but the prophecy that Jehoiakim's line would come to a bad end was fulfilled when Zedekiah was taken as a prisoner to Babylon.

This passage is sometimes read on Bible Sunday, and it certainly throws interesting light on one aspect of the story of 'how we got our Bible'. Only when there are real obstacles in the way, or when there is a danger of the message being forgotten, does prophecy have to be committed to writing. Even then it is meant to be read *aloud*. The phrase '*there were added besides unto them many like words*' (verse 32) means that the second scroll was fuller than the first, or that the prophet had later messages written down as there was opportunity. But it may also serve as a reminder to us of the debt that we owe to the scribes, to the editors who collected and arranged and preserved the sayings and doings of the prophets. These editors '*added*' to the words of the great prophets '*many like words*,' derived sometimes from other prophets whose names we cannot know, and derived at other times from the editors' own response to the message of the prophets, and from their own understanding of the word of God. See H. H. Rowley, *The Growth of the Old Testament*, chapter IX.

Parallels may be drawn between this story and similar happenings in the lives of Tyndale, Luther and Bunyan. The first copies of Tyndale's New Testament were bought up and burnt, but the money paid for them made possible a cheaper edition in better type. Jeremiah's time of hiding was fruitful, like Luther's stay in the Wartburg, and Bunyan's in Bedford gaol.

One of the first Christian heretics, Marcion, was accused of 'criticising with a penknife'. He cut out the OT from the Bible, and also many parts of the NT which did not fit in with his beliefs. There is always the temptation for us to ignore those parts of Scripture which do not square with our own theories. We have our own quiet way of doing what Jehoiakim, and Marcion, did so brazenly, with the highest of motives. We tone down, or ignore, passages which conflict with what we want to do, or with our doctrinal or ecclesiastical prejudices. So it becomes harder for the Lord to bring His Church into that unity which is His will. This is one reason why it is good for preachers to follow the 'Christian year', since this may compel us to make sermons on the subjects we would prefer to leave on one side. We may reject parts of God's word that are not palatable to us or to our congregations, but they still are there. We may turn a blind eye and a deaf ear to them, but still they stand. Books can be destroyed by burning, and ideas by neglect; but not the word of God.

37¹⁻²¹: Jeremiah is imprisoned

After the Babylonians had withdrawn for a time from the siege of Jerusalem in the reign of Zedekiah, the prophet set out to visit Anathoth. He was arrested on a charge of trying to desert to the enemy. After he had been imprisoned for several days, the king sent secretly for him. After telling the king that he is certain to be captured by the enemy, the prophet pleads not to be sent back to the prison. Instead he is put in the guard's courtyard, and is allotted a ration of food until supplies run out.

37¹. '*Zedekiah*' is of course '*the son of Josiah*', '*whom Nebuchadrezzar king of Babylon made king*'.

37³. '*Zephaniah*'. Cf. **21¹⁻²**.

37⁵. '*Pharaoh's army*'. The Pharaoh was Hophra; cf. **34²¹**, **44³⁰**.

37⁶⁻¹⁰. See Lamentations **4¹⁷⁻²⁰**.

37¹⁰. See **26⁶**, which is probably twenty years earlier.

37¹². '*to receive his portion*'. This is not easy to understand. It has been suggested that the reference is to a yearly allocation by lot of plots of common ground, but this hardly seems to be likely when the invaders were still in the land.

37¹³. '*a captain of the ward*'. Better, 'a sentry' (*RSV*).
'*thou fallest away*'. The prophet is accused of deserting to the Babylonians.

37¹⁵. '*Jonathan the scribe*'. Cf. **36¹²**.
'*they had made that the prison*'. Perhaps because the usual prison had been damaged, or was needed for other purposes during the siege.

37¹⁶. '*the dungeon house*'. Cf. **38⁶**.

This incident is much later than chapter **36**, but about the same period as **34⁸⁻²²**. The prophet had no intention of leaving the city permanently; he was no rat leaving a sinking ship. Yet the suspicion that he may be going over to the Chaldeans is very natural (cf. **38²**). The angry officials have him flogged and flung into a dungeon (verse 15). They hold that his exhortations are irresponsible, even though their own pet prophets have been proved wrong at last (verse 19). Zedekiah suspects that the Lord may be speaking by Jeremiah, but can summon up neither the faith nor the will to obey. So his fears and his anxiety lead him to take, or drift into, the way to sure disaster. There may have been considerable similarities in temperament between the prophet and his king; where they differed was that the prophet was prepared to draw his strength from God (see verse 17). The prisoner who is a servant of the Lord is far stronger than the king who is a slave to wishful thinking and self-deception (cf. verse 9).

Once more we see the amazing boldness which God's strength supplies to His prophet. One is reminded of Luther's saying, 'It is more comforting to have God for a friend than to have the friendship of the whole world'. There are all too many examples in the world today, and in recent history, of men put into dungeons or worse places for their loyalty to God: see for example Dietrich Bonhoeffer's *Letters and Papers from Prison* (Fontana). These men find, as Jeremiah did, that the word of the Lord continues to come to His servants, even in their dungeons (cf. verses 16-17). They deserve the tribute that once was paid to John Knox, 'He feared God so much that he never feared the face of any man'. See Phil 1¹²⁻¹³.

38¹⁻¹³: 'An enemy of the people'

The imprisoned prophet persists in advising people to surrender to the enemy, and the officials therefore demand his execution. They have him thrown into an underground water tank which is deep in mud, and leave him there to die of starvation. But an Ethiopian eunuch gets permission from the king to take Jeremiah out of the cistern, and he is allowed to return to the guard's courtyard.

38². '*his life shall be unto him for a prey*'. The only spoils of war that will come to him are that he will be left with what he stands up in—but he will be alive, '*he will live*'. Cf. **21⁹, 39¹⁸, 45⁵**.

38⁶. '*dungeon*'. See *RV*m. An underground water cistern (cf. **2¹³**, Lam 3⁵³).
    '*the king's son*'. See commentary on **36²⁶**.

38⁷. '*sitting in the gate*'. The city gate was the usual place for dealing with disputes and petitions.

38⁹. '*he is like to die*'. The Hebrew says 'he is dead' (see *RV*m). In other words, 'he is as good as dead', unless something is done about it.

This seems to be later than chapter **37** for now the bread is all gone and people are eating whatever else they can find (verse 9; cf. **37**[21]). But the prophet has not been singing the song of him whose bread he ate (verse 2). Rather than be a traitor, either to God or to his own nation, he lays himself open to a charge of treason. The king, like Pilate washing his hands, leaves the prophet to be dealt with by the pro-Egyptian royal officials (verse 5). They see that Jeremiah is put out of the way. The incident may have taken place towards the end of the dry season when there would be little but mud left in the cistern (verse 6).

But there is a '*son of Ham*', a slave, one of that despised nation on whom the curse of God was supposed to lie. This 'gentile' has the courage to urge the King to act and frustrate the injustice and cruelty of his powerful courtiers. This Ebed-melech takes '*thirty men*' with him, in case there is any trouble (verse 10. Notice, however, that one Hebrew manuscript has 'three men', and see *RSV*). They get some old clothes and rags from the palace stores (this seems to be the meaning of verse 11; cf. *RSV*), so that they are able to rescue the prophet in the way least likely to cause him injury. This was an extremely dangerous errand of mercy, since it was carried out in defiance of powerful men, against whom the king himself could not '*do any thing*' (verse 5). What led this foreigner to help Jeremiah, we are not told. But his behaviour led the prophet to understand that, just as the Lord can use a heathen emperor to punish His people, so also He may have among the Gentiles some who have put their '*trust in*' Himself (see **39**[18]). God is ready to reward them, just as he rewards any who will be faithful in Judah. See commentary below on **39**[15-18]. Cf. **45**[5].

38[14-28]: The final message to Zedekiah

The king sends secretly for the prophet to ask his advice, and promises not to allow Jeremiah to be executed. But the word of the Lord is still that it is only if the king surrenders that Jerusalem can be spared.

38[14]. '*the third entry*'. This cannot be identified, but it was a place where the prophet could meet the king secretly. See note on verse 27.

38¹⁷. '*princes*'. Again, these are officials. Also in verse 25.

38²¹. '*shewed*'. He has had a vision of the palace women singing a dirge for Zedekiah.

38²². '*set thee on*'. Follow *RV*m.

38²³. '*wives*'. The royal harem; cf. Deut 17¹⁷.

38²⁷. '*the matter was not perceived*'. The prophet and the king had not been overheard.

Here we have another vivid demonstration of the weakness of Zedekiah's character. The king knows that he is powerless to '*do anything against*' his leading men, and his promise not to give Jeremiah '*into the hand*' of those who seek the prophet's life cannot have been worth very much. Then Zedekiah confesses that he could never face the taunts of those of his countrymen who, either on grounds of prudence or in obedience to Jeremiah's message, have already gone over to the Babylonians. Once the king has secured a word of the Lord from the prophet, he makes it clear that his promise not to allow Jeremiah to be put to death is conditional. It depends on the prophet maintaining complete silence about what has passed between them (verse 24). The king is even more afraid of his leading men than he is of bearing the responsibility for the destruction of Jerusalem (verses 23, 25).

Here is a situation worthy of all the skill of the most brilliant playwright, for on the other hand we have Jeremiah. He has scarcely had time to realize that, at any rate for the time being, he has been saved from a death through starvation, exhaustion and suffocation. He has scarcely had the time to clean off the mire of the cistern, or to get rid of the smell that clings to him, and yet he is now warning the king that it is his feet that will soon be '*sunk in the mire*' (verse 22), unless he heeds the warning that the Lord has sent through His prophet. Zedekiah may be the one who speaks about the living God (verse 16), but it is Jeremiah who serves Him. However eagerly the prophet may have wished to tell his king pleasing things, he cannot. He gives the advice for which he is asked, not on grounds of prudence or self-preservation, not as a matter of shrewd statesmanship or military strategy, but in the name of

the Lord (verses 17, 21). In what the prophet says there may
be heard '*the voice of the Lord*' (verse 20). Drama is certainly
here, and it is not fiction but authentic fact.

Some writers have argued that Jeremiah was wrong to
conceal from his enemies, the leading officials, the full import
of this interview with the king. He was not far removed from
his flogging or from the darkness, filth and hunger of the cistern
and, whether or not he was in the wrong, we should never have
known about it if the facts had not been recorded either by
Jeremiah himself, or by his admirers. What is important is
not the example of the prophet, but the word of the Lord.
There are some relevant and important pages on 'telling the
truth' in Dietrich Bonhoeffer's *Ethics* (SCM Press).

39¹⁻¹⁴: The fall of Jerusalem

When Jerusalem fell, Zedekiah's sons were executed, and the
king himself was blinded and taken to Babylon, along with
all the more wealthy of his subjects. Jeremiah was set free by
the Chaldeans, and put under the protection of Gedaliah.

39³. '*Nergal-sharezer*', etc. See *RV*m.
   '*princes*'. Better, 'officials'.

39⁴. '*the gate betwixt the two walls*'. This was probably in the
south-east of the city.
   '*the Arabah*'. The southern part of the Jordan valley.

39⁴⁻⁷. Cf. Lamentations, chapter 4.

39⁵. '*Riblah*'. In Syria; Nebuchadrezzar's headquarters for
the campaign. Cf. 2 Kings 23³³.

39⁸. '*burned*'. Cf. 38²³.

Verses 11-14 do not tally in some respects with **40¹⁻⁶**, and
chapter **40** (which is possibly from Baruch) is probably more
accurate. This whole section is related to 2 Kings 25¹⁻¹² and
to **52⁴⁻¹⁶**. So the worshippers of Nergal and Nebo (see the
names in verse 3) were used by the Lord, and the last king of
Judah became a blinded prisoner (verse 7; cf. Ezek 12¹⁰⁻¹³).
Jeremiah chooses to remain '*among the people*', to dwell among

'*the poor of the people, which had nothing, in the land of Judah*' (verses 14, 10). He goes where it seems 'right' to go (see *RV*m 40⁴) and supports the new leader, Gedaliah, who is the son of his friend Ahikam (verse 14; cf. 26²⁴).

This was the end of Judah and the end of an epoch. The end of an age, such as this, is a forerunner of the final end, at the Coming of the Lord Jesus Christ. We do not like reminders such as this that the works of man are destructible. But the gospel speaks, as the prophets did, of a peace that lies only on the other side of the destruction of sin. This is not to deny that men are responsible for their acts. It may seem that Jerusalem, and Zedekiah, got 'what was coming to them'. God may use the savagery of the enemy to punish the sin of His people, but that is not to say that He is responsible for that savagery. Instead of permitting the logic of sin to lead to death, God intervenes with His grace to turn the evil of men to His purpose of salvation. He is the First and the Last; He inaugurated history and will bring it to the End He has ordained. But still we are like those of whom Jesus said 'they ate and drank and married . . . and they knew nothing until the flood came and swept them all away'. He also said 'As things were in Noah's days, so will they be when the Son of Man comes' (Mt 24³⁷⁻⁹, *NEB*). It is natural to feel sorry for Zedekiah; it is even more important to heed the warnings that come to ourselves, while there is time.

39¹⁵⁻¹⁸: The promise to Ebed-melech

The prophet is sent to the African who rescued him from the cistern to assure him that God will reward him.

39¹⁵. '*the court of the guard*'. See 38¹³, ²⁸.

39¹⁷. '*the men of whom thou art afraid*'. This could refer to the Chaldeans, but is more likely to mean the '*princes*', the powerful men at the court of Zedekiah.

39¹⁸. '*the sword*'. This does refer to the Chaldeans.

Once it became clear that no notice would be taken of the advice that the government of Judah should surrender to

Nebuchadrezzar, Jeremiah is sent to Ebed-melech to assure his rescuer that the Lord will save him, not only from the officials whose enmity he had incurred through helping the prophet, but also from the Chaldeans when they capture Jerusalem. Part of his reward will be to see God's word fulfilled when the city falls, for he has helped a prophet in the name of a prophet. But above all, his life will be spared, because he has put his '*trust*' in '*the Lord*' (verse 18).

The name '*Ebed-melech*' means simply 'servant of the king' and the Ethiopian was a good servant of Zedekiah when he persuaded the king to permit the rescue of the prophet. But Zedekiah was no faithful servant of the King of Kings, whereas the Ethiopian was. Zedekiah refused to '*trust*' in the Lord and fell to his enemies; Ebed-melech trusted in God, and God delivered him from his enemies (cf. Josh 2⁹, ¹⁴).

We have here an important illustration of the 'missionary message of the Old Testament' which is to blossom into the wider insights of the 'Second Isaiah' and the book of Jonah (cf. Gen 18²⁵, Heb 10³⁸, Acts 9²⁷, ³⁶⁻⁸). There have been situations within the last few years in the Congo and in the Mau-mau area of Kenya where Africans have risked their own lives by helping the servants of God to escape. Like Ebed-melech (whom we know simply by his job—'royal servant'), many of them were anonymous.

40¹-41¹⁸: Gedaliah

At first Jeremiah is put with other prisoners of war, but then he is allowed to go free. He joins Gedaliah, the new governor, at Mizpah. Gedaliah ignores a warning and so Ishmael is able to succeed with his plan to assassinate the governor.

40⁵. '*while he was not yet gone back*'. Better, with *RSV*, 'if you remain'.

40⁶. '*Mizpah*'. To the north of Jerusalem, on the main road to Shechem.

40⁷. '*fields*'. Better 'open country', outside the towns and villages.

41¹. '*the seventh month*'. The year is not given, but '*the eleventh year of Zedekiah*' may be intended (cf. **39²**). But see also **52³⁰**.

41⁴. '*the second day after*'. By our reckoning, this is the 'next day'.

41⁵. '*their beards shaven and their clothes rent*'. These were signs that they were in mourning for the fate of their country. They came from places that had all been famous once, and had all been ruined: '*the house of the Lord*' in Jerusalem had also been ruined.

41⁸. '*hidden in the field*'. Secreted in storage pits in the open country. Cf. **40⁷**.

41⁹. '*the pit . . . which Asa the king had made*'. Perhaps an underground cistern for storing water. This may be linked with 1 Kings 15²⁰⁻².

41¹⁰. '*king's daughters*'. Women of royal blood are always important in a time of revolt.

41¹². '*the great waters*'. Probably a large reservoir (cf. 2 Sam 2¹³).

41¹⁴. '*cast about*'. Better, they 'turned back'.

41¹⁷. '*Geruth Chimham*'. This was a khan,—an inn, a lodging place (see *RV*m and cf. **9²**).

'*The word which came to Jeremiah from the Lord*' (**40¹**) is a curious phrase in this context. As it stands it can apply only to what is said to the prophet by the '*captain of the guard*' (**40²⁻⁵**), and we have the unusual situation of the word of the Lord being spoken to a prophet by a Gentile military commander! So the prophet goes to Mizpah, the fortress four or five miles to the northwest of Jerusalem, which Asa had once fortified to protect Judah against attacks from Israel (1 Kings 15²²). When the refugees began to flock together there '*out of all places whither they were driven*' (**40¹²**), they were urged to settle down free from anxiety, and get on with the really urgent business of providing themselves with food (cf. **40¹⁰**). Many of them must have recognized, as Johanan did, that Gedaliah alone stood between the little that remained of Judah and complete extinction (**40¹⁵**). But Ishmael, who was of royal blood, was prepared to envy Gedaliah, who was not. Ishmael did not find it hard to gain support from Baalis, king of Ammon, since Ammon had no desire to see a revived Judah standing between her and the Mediterranean. She probably had hopes rather of adding at least some of the land of Judah to her own territory (**40¹⁴**).

So Ishmael murders Gedaliah, and his crime is the more dreadful since he had eaten with Gedaliah, and only on the previous day (**41¹**). A day after the assassination, Ishmael pretends to share the grief of a group of eighty men who are on their way to sacrifice in the ruins of Jerusalem, but then proceeds to have them killed. He is then able to force those who have gathered round Gedaliah in Mizpah, including the women of royal descent, to go with him on the way to Ammon (**41¹⁰**). But Johanan rescues these people before they reach the frontier. He is, however, afraid to return to Mizpah, and the party now moves in the direction of Egypt (**41¹⁸**). The last hope of Judah seems to have gone, and they reach their last resting place in Judah—an inn near Bethlehem. Ishmael has done the damage, and nothing further is heard of him.

Jeremiah had been guided to refuse honourable treatment in Babylon, and now he goes with this sorry remnant of his nation, deeper into misery and degradation. He is their only hope, because he still serves the Lord who hid him from the sword of Ishmael.

As the note on **41¹** above suggests, it is difficult to decide what period of time is covered by this section (cf. 2 Kings 25²²⁻⁶). Gedaliah may have fallen within three months of the destruction of Jerusalem. If this is so, the Chaldean experiment with Judah as a province of the Baylonian empire, under a leader from Judah who was not of the royal line, was very short-lived. If the deportation of **52³⁰** was a reprisal for the assassination of Gedaliah and his Chaldean bodyguard, Gedaliah may have had about three years in power. But reprisals have been known to be belated. Moreover, the event mentioned in **52³⁰** cannot be certainly linked with the murder of Gedaliah.

42¹-43⁷: The flight into Egypt

Johanan and his group ask the prophet for an oracle from the
Lord. After ten days, Jeremiah says that the Lord's will is,
that they shall remain in Judah. There is nothing to fear
from the Chaldean authorities, whereas if they go to Egypt
they will all die. But Johanan and his followers refuse to
accept this as a word of the Lord. They go to Egypt and
compel the prophet to accompany them.

43⁷. '*Tahpanhes*'. The northernmost fortified city of Egypt.
Cf. **2¹⁶.**

Although they have already begun to move towards Egypt
(**41¹⁷**), these people ask Jeremiah to pray to *his* God. He
reminds them firmly that his God is also *their* God, the Lord
who has covenanted with them. The point goes home, at least
so far as their way of talking is concerned: '*thy God*' (**42²**)
'*your God*' (**42⁴**), '*our God*' (**42⁶**). (Cf. 'this thy son' and 'this
thy brother' in Lk 15³⁰, ³².) The prophet is no diviner with a
magic technique to conjure up an oracle at will: he has to
wait until the Lord gives him a word to deliver (cf. **28¹¹⁻¹²**).
After '*ten days*' he tells them that the murder of Gedaliah has
not made it any the less important for them to remain in
Judah. God's purpose does not change, though His method
alters as circumstances alter. (This is the meaning of '*I repent
me*' in **42¹⁰**; see commentary on **18¹⁻¹²**). But just as they would
not listen to the Lord when He was about to '*break down*'
and '*destroy*', so they will not listen now when His will is '*to
build, and to plant*' (cf. **1¹⁰**). They are still set on going astray,
even at the cost of their lives (see *RSV* of **42²⁰**). They think
that they are cheating the Lord, but they are really cheating
themselves; instead of running away from trouble, they are
running into it (**42¹⁶**). To provide themselves with an excuse,
they allege that the prophet ought to say, 'Thus says Baruch'
instead of '*Thus saith the Lord*'. But although they claim to
doubt Jeremiah's integrity, they drag the prophet off with
them, perhaps in a pathetic attempt to keep God's favour
even while they are acting in flat contradiction of His word
(**43⁸**). Still despised and still rejected, the prophet is forced to be
acquainted still with grief.

This was the complete end of Judah. All those whom the

L

Lord wished to remain in their own land went into Egypt,
and did not return (43⁴⁻⁶, cf. 42¹⁷). The people that had
become a nation centuries before by the act of their Saviour
in leading them out of bondage in Egypt, now ceases to be a
people by turning its back on the Lord and defiantly going
back into Egypt. The Lord can act in Egypt still, and He will
give them no future there. It is as if the 'bad figs' (chapter 24)
had themselves jumped into the dustbin. Of course there were
still some peasants left in the former territory of God's people,
even after the deportation of 582 BC (52³⁰), but these were to
become the 'Samaritans'. Then there were the exiles in Babylon,
but it was only a madman like Jeremiah who could dare to
believe now that the Lord would bring His Jonah out of the
belly of that great fish.

The group led by Johanan is an example of people, in a condition even more desperate than they realize, who are playing
at prayer, instead of meaning sincerely, 'Thy will be done'.
The prophet alone is genuinely prepared to wait on God, even
if days have to pass before His will is clearly known. Although
the prophet's warnings have been proved right over and over
again, in the disasters from which they escaped only by the
skin of their teeth, still the people of Judah have not learned.
Whatever they say, their behaviour shows that. The only
proper way to want to know the will of God is to want to
obey that will, and not merely to take it into account as one
possibility among others. Like this pathetic group of displaced
persons, we are in a world where it is tempting to seek with all
our hearts for security (cf. 42¹⁴), instead of seeking first the
will of God. However 'natural' this may be, it is wrong, and
foolish, and very dangerous. To reject the will of God, especially when it has been clearly made known to us, is to sin
against ourselves (42²⁰⁻¹); this is part of the danger of listening
to sermons, whether as a preacher or a member of a congregation. 'Thy will be done' does not make for an easy
life. But the opposite does not put anyone out of reach of
sorrow and suffering either, and it cuts us off from the only
Energy with which these troubles may be met victoriously.

43⁸⁻¹³: A sign in Egypt

The prophet hides large stones at the entrance of the Pharaoh's lodge in Tahpanhes, as a sign from the Lord that the king of Babylon will set his throne there when he invades and punishes Egypt.

43⁹. '*great stones*'. These are to serve as a pedestal for the invader's throne. See *RV*m.

43¹⁰. '*pavilion*', i.e. 'canopy'.

43¹². '*he shall array himself . . . his garment*'. The picture is of a shepherd getting the lice out of his cloak (not putting it on); Nebuchadrezzar will pick Egypt clean. See *RSV*.
    '*in peace*'. Better, 'victorious'.

43¹³. '*the pillars of Beth-shemesh*'. These were the 'obelisks' of 'Heliopolis' (see *RV*m). One of these is the 'Cleopatra's Needle' that stands now on the Thames Embankment in London; another stands in Central Park, New York.

For the time being, the Lord has decided that nothing shall withstand the might of Babylon (verses 10-11; cf. **27⁶, 15²**). Again the prophet warns Johanan and his group, this time in an acted parable, that they are certainly not safe in Egypt. Nebuchadrezzar 'shall clean the land of Egypt, as a shepherd cleans his cloak of vermin' (verse 12 in *RSV*), and shall go away unscathed. There is no frontier beyond which the Lord's word does not run (cf. Ps 139⁷⁻¹²). Nebuchadrezzar invaded Egypt in 586 BC (see Ezek 29¹⁹⁻²⁰, 30¹⁰⁻¹²), but he did not attempt to incorporate it in his empire. Punishment was sufficient, and Babylon was not troubled by Egypt again.

44¹⁻³⁰: Prophesying in Egypt

The Lord tells the prophet to rebuke the people from Judah for continuing to sacrifice to heathen gods in Egypt, and to warn them of the horrors that are coming upon them.

44¹. '*Pathros*'. This is in the south of Egypt, while the other places mentioned are in the north.

44³. '*burn incense*'. Better, 'offer sacrifice'. See also verses 5, 8, 15, etc.

44⁹. '*in the streets*'. Cf. **7**¹⁶⁻²⁰.

44¹⁹. '*cakes*'. These possibly were shaped to resemble the goddess, or made like a star which was her symbol. See *TWB*, 98.

44³⁰. '*them that seek his life*'. The Pharaoh (Hophra) was strangled by Egyptian assassins in 569 or 564 B C.

At the end of what we know of the prophet's life, the same things are true as at the beginning; Judah is still rebellious (verse 16) and the Lord is still wakeful to perform His word ('*I watch*', verse 27; cf. **1**¹²). The '*queen of heaven*' (verses 17-19, 25) is Anath (Ishtar) who became linked with 'Diana of the Ephesians' at a much later stage (cf. 2 Kings 21³⁻⁵, 23⁵, ¹¹⁻¹², Acts 19²⁷⁻²⁸). Her cult gave a more prominent place to women than did the worship of the Lord, and this accounts for the part the women take in the dispute.

Verse 17 is most important as evidence of the continued apostasy of Israel through centuries. Clearly the majority of people regarded the reforms of Josiah as an innovation, and they dated all their troubles from the time of his attempts to make them turn to Yahweh alone in their worship. The 'religion of Israel' was heathenism, not very different from the religion of neighbouring tribes: faith in the Lord was never more than a minority's way of life in Canaan. This is why the prophets look back with longing to the wilderness period. It was a very long time before many people would agree that it is the Lord who 'maketh the Pleiades and Orion' (Amos 5⁹), and, for that matter, Venus and all the rest of the stars. Every complaint the prophets made about Israel's flagrant and un-natural rebellion against her Deliverer is based on the facts as they knew them. Not only to the group with Johanan, but also to representatives of the Jews who had been in Egypt for a long time previously (verse 1), Jeremiah is reiterating what has been said by their prophets from Hosea on; it is fatal for the Lord's covenant people to worship other gods. While they persist in doing so the Lord must '*watch over them*', wherever they are, '*for evil, and not for good*' (verse 27). See also **7**²⁵⁻²⁶, **19**⁴.

The end of Judah's representatives in Egypt is quite certain, though the prophet is represented here as being prepared to allow that a few individuals may escape from Egypt (verses 14, 28). We do not know where or when Jeremiah died. Was he still alive to see the fulfilment of his prophecy when the Pharaoh Hophra was assassinated? This is the last of his recorded prophecies. He ends as he began, brave and loyal to his Lord, with warnings of disaster for an 'adulterous generation' who could learn nothing but the wrong lessons, even from catastrophe (verse 18). Even when people have reached the stage of calling good evil, and calling evil good, the prophet of the Lord stays with them. Even when they have reached the stage of looking back to the days of Manasseh as 'the good old days' (cf. verse 17), the Lord in His patience still sends them His word. Our last view of Jeremiah is of a man gifted with amazing courage, holding forth to people whom any 'reasonable' man would have left to go to their doom long before. We are reminded of the Source of his steadfastness and compassion and boldness in chapter **45**.

There is no conclusive answer to the argument of these Jews in Egypt. What is at stake here is—faith. The prophet had faith in God: the Jews had not. They looked back on the time of Manasseh as a period when they had '*plenty of victuals, and were well, and saw no evil*' (verse 17). History is no revelation of the power of the true God to any one who is without faith. Jeremiah died in faith. He had no family to carry on his name; he had no hope of a resurrection. He was content to leave everything to God, to the One in whose fellowship class he had shared for a time. All he can say on behalf of the Lord is that the time will come when the Jews '*shall know whose word shall stand, mine, or theirs*' (verse 28). The debate continues, and those who side with Jeremiah can only say in word and deed, 'I believe in God . . .'.

45¹⁻⁵: Concerning Baruch

The Lord tells the prophet that Baruch must not expect any reward save that of knowing that his life will be preserved.

45¹. '*the fourth year of Jehoiakim*'. We are back again in time at the point when Baruch worked with the prophet on the preparation of the written version of his prophecies (see **36¹**; cf. **25¹**, **46²**).

This oracle 'concerning' Baruch (*RV*m of verse 2) may have been included at the end of the record of the doings of Jeremiah as a modest postscript by Baruch himself. The promise of the Lord to him was fulfilled and he was with the prophet at least until the time when they were dragged off together into Egypt (43³, ⁶). This '*Baruch the son of Neriah*' may have been a brother of '*Seraiah the son of Neriah*' who held high office at the court of Zedekiah (51⁵⁹). There was no prospect of any such respected position in international and national politics for Baruch. Instead, he has become involved with a true prophet of the Lord. After all the trouble and suffering of writing out, and then reading in public, messages concerning the ruin of his own nation, Baruch finds it unbearable that his reward seems to be that he is outlawed. Any ambitions he may have had must now be abandoned, and he has to learn for himself, as the prophet has already been learning for years, that fellowship with the Lord and with His servants is fellowship in '*great things*', because it is fellowship in suffering (cf. 12⁵, 15¹⁹). So the Lord puts to Baruch the question, 'When *I* must destroy what *I* built, and when *I* must uproot what *I* planted, will *you* look for great things for *yourself*?' (cf. verses 4-5). Baruch must learn to understand God's sorrow in having to destroy for righteousness' sake the plant that He Himself sowed and has nourished. Then he will find that there is no place for his own complaint. God Himself is having to surrender His hopes for His own people, so it is not surprising that His servants may have to surrender their little hopes. It must be, and it is, enough that God is the living God, and that we are alive (cf. verse 5). Out of the wreck of God's people Baruch's life will be saved; he will be a brand plucked from the burning and that will be enough (cf. Mt 6³³).

So the Son of God calls men to 'take up the cross daily' and promises nothing besides 'tribulation', except the one thing that matters—life, 'life in abundance'. So we say in the Methodist *Covenant Service*, 'let me be employed for Thee, or laid aside for Thee; exalted for Thee, or brought low for Thee . . . I freely and heartily yield all things to Thy pleasure and disposal' (cf. 1 Cor 15³⁶).

'*Thus far are the words of Jeremiah*': these words from 51⁶⁴ might well come at this point, since chapters **46-52** are a kind of appendix to the account of God's dealings with Jeremiah and with Judah. This appendix is a collection of oracles concerning other nations and is intended to illustrate Jeremiah's work as a prophet to the nations (see 1⁵, 25¹³).

The State of Judah was at an end. Israel was scattered among the nations (cf. Deut 28⁶⁴). Jerusalem's walls were flattened, the Temple destroyed, the city burned. All the old ideas and beliefs seemed to be shattered. Jeremiah had been proved right in his warnings, but what then? The gods of Babylon seemed to have triumphed most convincingly and it is amazing that Yahweh's people were not swallowed up, as other little nations were, and submerged for ever as a people. But as men began to shake themselves conscious once more, after the numbness of defeat, the seed that God had sown in the work of His prophet began to bear real fruit. It began to dawn on a few Jews that Jeremiah had been right in his insistence that the past history of God's people, and their present suffering, could be understood in the light of the sovereign design of the Lord who can be trusted to vindicate His purposes. There remained still the hope of a new community, loyal to the calling of the Lord who was still their covenant-God. There could be a new Exodus in His good time, more glorious than the Exodus from Egypt. The future was still in God's hand, He was still the Saviour and would make with His people a new covenant, the expression of His everlasting love.

III. Prophecies concerning the nations (46¹-51⁶⁴)

46¹⁻²⁸: Concerning Egypt

46¹. '*concerning the nations*'. This verse is the title to chapters **46-51**.

46². '*Carchemish*'. Nebuchadrezzar's success in forcing the Egyptians to retreat in 605 B C was one of the turning points of history, for it made it certain that the Chaldeans would succeed the Assyrians as the dominant empire of the time. This Babylonian success in repulsing the Egyptians may have shown Jeremiah for the first time the identity of the foe that he knew would come from the '*north*'. See also 2 Kings 24⁷.

46⁵. '*terror*'. Cf. 6²⁵, 20³, ¹⁰.

46⁶. '*Euphrates*'. This is where the Egyptians have met with trouble. The prophet now knows that the foe from the '*north*' lives by this river.

46⁹. '*Cush*', '*Put*' and '*Ludim*' are the allies of Egypt.

46¹⁴. '*Noph*'. This is Memphis, the capital of Egypt in those times.

46¹⁵. '*strong ones*'. Follow *RV*m. The 'strong one' is Apis, the sacred bull of Egypt.

46¹⁶. '*to our own people*'. Egypt relied considerably on mercenary soldiers.

46¹⁸. '*Tabor*', '*Carmel*'. Nebuchadrezzar is likened to a mighty mountain.

46²⁰. '*destruction*'. See *RV*m and read with *RSV*, 'a gadfly from the north has come upon her'.

46²¹. '*calves of the stall*'. The mercenaries are like 'fatted calves', out of trim for campaigning.

46²². Follow *RV*m. The '*serpent*' is hurrying away in terror. The serpent was conspicuous in the royal insignia of Egypt and is therefore an appropriate symbol for that country.

46²³. '*cannot be searched*', because it is impenetrable.

46²⁵. '*Amon*'. The chief god of '*No*' (Thebes).

46²⁷⁻²⁸. See 30¹⁰⁻¹¹ where these verses are in context, as *RV*m suggests.

Some of these prophecies about the nations are in verse—see chapters **46-51** in *RSV*. For information on many details it will be necessary to use a larger commentary, and a good Scripture atlas will prove useful here too. The grouping of these prophecies is dependent on **25**[19-26]. See commentary there.

These oracles on Egypt belong to the time when it became clear that Chaldea was to be the top power in the prophet's world. The Egyptian expedition's rout from Carchemish dealt a heavy blow to that country's prestige. When eventually Nebuchadrezzar invaded Egypt (verse 13; cf. **48**[8-13]) and pursued a 'scorched earth' policy, it could be claimed that the Lord had overthrown the gods of Egypt. Egypt's sin was pride (cf. verse 8), and where there is pride a fall is sure to follow.

47[1-7]: Concerning the Philistines

47[1]. *'Gaza'*. The capital of Philistia. If the meaning of the editors in grouping the oracles as they do in these chapters was that all these territories—Philistia, Moab, Ammon, etc.—will suffer at the hands of the victorious Chaldeans, the reference to Gaza being punished by the *'Pharaoh'* seems to be rather out of place. The Philistine capital could have been attacked by the Egyptians before they were driven back from Carchemish. But the oracle has to do with an attack by the Chaldeans. See verse 2.

47[2]. *'the north'* here stands for Babylonia.

47[4]. *'Tyre and Zidon'*. These belong to Phoenicia, but may be mentioned here as allies of Philistia.

'Caphtor'. This is Crete, which is believed to be the original home of the Philistines (cf. Amos 9[7], Ezek 25[15-16]).

47[5]. *'Baldness'*. To shave the head and *'cut'* one's self were conventional signs of mourning (see **41**[5], **48**[37], **16**[6]).

'their valley'. This is the 'plain' of Philistia. *RSV* has 'remnant of the Anakim' on the basis of the *LXX*; the Anakim, the giants who had once lived in Palestine, were believed to be ancestors of the Philistines (cf. Josh 11[21-2], Num 13[22, 28, 33]).

48[1-47]: Concerning Moab

Unlike the prophecy on Philistia, this prophecy on Moab shows signs of considerable 'borrowing' from sources other than Jeremiah (see Amos 2[1-3], Zeph 2[8-11], Isa 15[1]-16[12],

26¹⁰⁻¹², Ezek 25⁸⁻¹¹). Moab joined in the attack on Judah when Jehoiakim revolted against Nebuchadrezzar. Moabites were among the representatives of the neighbouring states who came to Judah early in the reign of Zedekiah (see **12¹⁻¹³**, **27¹⁻¹¹**, 2 Kings 24²). It is therefore not unlikely that Jeremiah delivered prophecies concerning her, and these may form the nucleus of this chapter.

48¹. '*Nebo*', '*Kiriathaim*'. These were on the eastern frontier of Moab, to the east of the Dead Sea.
'*Misgab*'. This should be 'the fortress' (cf. *RV*m).

48². '*Heshbon*'. Another Moabite town, and '*Madmen*' is possibly yet another.
'*let us cut her off*'. The aim is not plunder, but destruction, genocide.

48³. '*Horonaim*'. Another Moabite town, cf. verses 5, 34. (See Isa 15⁵ where the '*ascent of Luhith*' of verse 5 is also mentioned.)

48⁶. '*like the heath*'. Better, 'like the wild ass' (*RSV*). See **14⁶** and commentary there.

48⁷. '*works*'. These are 'fortifications' (*RSV*).

48⁸. '*the valley*' of the river Jordan.
'*the plain*'. The plateau of Moab. See reference in *RV*m.

48¹¹⁻¹². '*settled on his lees*'. Moab was famous for its wine· The metaphor here is that Moab needs to be '*emptied from vessel to vessel*' so that his '*scent*' may be '*changed*'. But the tilters who are coming to tilt him will empty his jars and break them to bits (cf. *RV*m). See Zephaniah 1¹². New wine was usually left to rest upon the sediment or the '*lees*' just long enough to preserve its '*taste*' and '*scent*' (see Isa 25⁶). If it was not then drawn off, it became syrupy, and more likely to go bad (cf. verses 32-3).

48¹³. '*Beth-el*'. This may here be the name of a god (cf. 1 Kings 12²⁸⁻⁹). 'El' was the principal god in Canaanite religion and

'Bethel' seems to have become a divine name in popular usage. But see also Amos 5⁴⁻⁶.

48²⁰. '*Arnon*'. The river on which the town of '*Aroer*' (verse 19) stood.

48²¹⁻⁴. A list of some of '*the cities of the land of Moab*'.

48²⁶. '*drunken*'. See 25¹⁵⁻¹⁶, ²⁷⁻⁹.

48²⁸. '*the hole's mouth*'. Better 'the mouth of a gorge' (*RSV*).

48²⁹⁻⁴⁶. This is an adaptation of passages from Isaiah, chapters 15-16, etc. See references in *RV*m. For verses 40-41, see **49²²**, where they seem to be in context.

48⁴⁷. Cf. 12¹⁵, 49⁶, ³⁹. '*Thus far . . .*'. An editorial conclusion to the whole collection.

The invader of Moab is not named, but we are probably meant to assume that it is the Chaldeans (see note on **47¹**). No explicit claim is made here that these oracles are '*the word of the Lord that came to Jeremiah the prophet*' (cf. **47¹**, **49³⁴**, **50¹**).

The sin of Moab is pride. This is stated over and over again in these prophecies. He must '*come down*' from his '*glory, and sit in*' the dust (verse 18) and it will be no longer possible for him to claim '*We are mighty men*' (verse 14). 'We have heard of the pride of Moab, that he is very proud; even of his arrogancy, and his pride, and his wrath; his boastings are nought' (Isa 15⁶). This pride shows itself in that '*he magnified himself against the Lord*' (verse 26); in that he '*trusted in*' his defence preparations and his '*treasures*' (verse 7); in that he trusts in idols (verse 13); and in that he is complacent and fond of comfort (verse 11). The arrogance and boasting and haughtiness of nations, or business groups, of trade unions or churches or individual human beings are all signs of a rebellion against God. It masks itself in many ways, but it is always essentially the same—a completely godless state of mind, living as if we had no Lord. It means acting as if we had

no one to please but ourselves; it means refusing to acknowledge that we have nothing that we did not receive. It means
acting as if it were true that 'I am the Captain of my soul'.
It is the attitude where we forget that, when we are really
up against it, it is no use relying on any idol, even if that idol
be Beth-el, the house of God, itself (verse 13; cf. 7¹⁻¹⁵, 26¹⁻⁶).
It means forgetting that, however great it may be, a man's
'wealth does not give him life' (Lk 12¹⁵, *NEB*). It leads a
man or a group to become '*settled on his lees*' (verse 11),
filled with apathy and inertia, with decorous, respectable
unbelief. This is the danger of comfortable groups in an
'affluent' society, a self-sufficient indifference, a syrupy wine
which is near to putrescence (cf. Ps 55¹⁹ in *AV*). Arnold
Toynbee reminds us in his *Study of History* that civilization
can only persist where there is a 'challenge' which meets with
an appropriate 'response'; blessed are those who have not
insulated themselves against the challenge of God, and who
are still permitted by Him to make the appropriate response
of humble, grateful faith. They can say with joy:

> *Pride of man and earthly glory,*
> *Sword and crown betray his trust:*
> *What with care and toil he buildeth,*
> *Tower and temple fall to dust.*
> *But God's power,*
> *Hour by hour,*
> *Is my temple and my tower.* (*MHB* 70)

Because the Son of God 'laid his glory by' and 'humbled
himself, and in obedience accepted even death—death on a
cross' (Phil 2⁸, *NEB*), there is hope even for Moab and the rest
of the proud of the earth (cf. verse 47). In Jesus Christ '*the
latter days*' have come when a change of fortune is possible
for those who put their faith in Him. Even though it once
seemed that Moab was a broken wine-jar for which no one
cared (cf. verse 38 and 22²⁸), the Potter still goes on working
the clay (cf. 18⁴). So we can be set free from slavery to trust
in the idol of our self-sufficiency, to find it eternally true that
His grace is sufficient for all our need.

49¹⁻⁶: Concerning the Ammonites

49¹. '*Malcam*'. This should be 'Milcom', the god of Ammon.

The verse appears to mean that Gad had been occupied by the Ammonites, possibly after the fall of the northern kingdom of '*Israel*'. The 'Ammonites' occupied the area around what is the modern city of Amman in Jordan.

49². '*Rabbah*'. The capital of Ammon, now called '*Amman*'.

49³. '*fences*'. Better, 'hedges' (*RSV*).

Once again the judgement is coming upon a people '*that trusted in her treasures*' (verse 4). This is the sin of these descendants of Lot: they glory '*in the valleys*', their rich fertile territory, and say '*Who shall come unto me?*', as if there were no God (verses 4-5). But they shall find that He is, first by knowing His punishment, and then by knowing His salvation (verses 5-6).

49⁷⁻²²: Concerning Edom

49⁸. '*inhabitants of Dedan*'. These were the commercial travellers of that period. Although their caravan routes usually pass through Edom, they are advised to keep away.

'*dwell deep*'. They are to withdraw into the remote wilderness to avoid becoming involved in the trouble that will come on the Edomites.

'*Esau*'. The ancestor of the Edomites.

49¹³. '*Bozrah*', the capital of Edom.

49¹⁶. '*dwellest in the clefts . . . holdest the height*'. Edom was almost inaccessible (cf. Obad 3).

49¹⁷. '*hiss*'. A sign of horror, not of disapproval.

49¹⁹. '*the pride of Jordan*'. See **12⁵** and comment there.

49¹⁹⁻²¹. This oracle recurs in **50⁴⁴⁻⁶** where it is in context.

No explicit claim is made that these oracles are the prophecies of Jeremiah. A comparison of verses 9-10 with Obadiah 5-6 and of verses 14-16 with Obadiah 1-4 suggests that *Obadiah* is the source of these passages, or that the editors of both books drew on a common source (see also Lam 4²¹, Ezek 25¹²⁻¹⁴, Ps 137⁷). Edom was quick to take advantage of the defeat of Judah when Jerusalem fell in 586 B C, and moved in to occupy territory within the borders of Judah. Therefore she must drink of the cup of the Lord's wrath (cf. 25¹⁷⁻²⁹). None of her rulers (see '*shepherd*' in verse 19) can '*stand before*' the Lion of Judah, the Lord who has a righteous concern to defend '*fatherless children*' and '*widows*' (verse 11). Again it is '*pride*' that will cause a people's downfall (verse 16), a pride whose symptoms were a false sense of security, self-sufficiency, wealth and wordly wisdom. Not till the time of John Hyrcanus (about 130 B C) did a Jewish leader assert the authority of Judah over the Edomites or Idumaeans. So it came about that an Idumaean was King in Jerusalem in the days when Jesus was born at Bethlehem.

49²³⁻⁷: Concerning Syria

49²³. '*Hamath*'. This is 110 miles to the north of Damascus.

'*Arpad*'. Yet another 95 miles to the north of '*Hamath*'. Again it is assumed that the Chaldean army is the Lord's instrument for punishing the nations. But the prophecy is not explicitly attributed to Jeremiah, and Syria is not in fact mentioned in the list of nations in 25¹⁷⁻²⁶. There is no evidence that Syria was invaded and defeated by the Chaldeans, though she submitted to Nebuchadrezzar in 605 B C.

49²⁷. Cf. Amos 1³⁻⁵.

'*Ben-hadad*'. The name of several of the kings of Syria (cf. 1 Kings 15¹⁸, ²⁰, 2 Kings 13²⁴).

49²⁸⁻³³: Concerning Kedar and Hazor

This poem deals with Arab tribes who are no match for the Chaldeans. They were noted for their peculiar way of cutting their hair (verse 32). They have been '*at ease*' and '*without care*', thinking they had no need of defence preparations (verse 31). They have been content to live as nomads, but they will be punished by the armies of Babylon. Again wealth and self-sufficiency are named as the cause of the downfall of these people. See 25²³⁻⁴, 9²⁵⁻⁶ (cf. Ezek 38¹⁰⁻¹¹).

49³⁴⁻⁹: Concerning Elam

49³⁴. This time the prophecy is explicitly attributed to Jeremiah and the editors date it at '*the beginning of the reign of Zedekiah*'.

'*Elam*'. The territory far to the east of Babylon, about 200 miles further to the east of Judah than Babylon itself. Elam later formed the nucleus of the Persian empire which overthrew the Babylonians (see Dan 8², Neh 1¹).

49³⁵. '*the bow*'. The Elamites were famous as skilled archers (cf. Isa 22⁶).

God's power to '*overthrow*' (1¹⁰, cf. verse 38) and also to 'build' (cf. verse 39) extends even as far as Elam, and those who are hoping that the Chaldeans, who have taken Jehoiachin away and put Zedekiah on the throne (cf. verse 34), will soon be overthrown by a rival far to the east, will find that they are mistaken.

50¹-51⁵⁸: Concerning Babylon, and the restoration of Israel and Judah

This anthology of sayings about Babylon includes a great deal of borrowing from other prophets, but may include some extracts from '*the word that the Lord spake . . . by Jeremiah*' (50¹). See references in *RV*m. 'The earth is the Lord's' and those who refuse to recognize this will be brought to see it sooner or later. Even the Chaldeans are not above the law. Because the Lord was prepared to use them as His instrument to punish others, that does not mean that they may do as they please and go scot-free. This is the main point of a rather confused group of oracles which, like some other parts of chapters **46-51,** may seem rather tedious. The *LXX* does not even attribute these sayings about Babylon to Jeremiah (see note on **51⁵⁸**).

51⁵⁹⁻⁶⁴ indicates that Jeremiah believed that the time would certainly come when the Lord would bring the power of Babylon to an end, but his main concern in asserting this was to discourage, and certainly not to rouse, hopes of a speedy end to the exile of the leading citizens of Judah. But the point of view of the oracles as they are now arranged in **50¹-51⁵⁸** is that of people who are living after the desecration of the

Jerusalem Temple (cf. 50²⁸, 51¹¹, ⁵¹) and who expect an early deliverance for the exiles (50¹⁷⁻¹⁹). There seems occasionally to be an attempt to imply that prophecies made by Jeremiah have now been fulfilled (compare 51²⁶ with 25¹², and 51⁴¹ with 25²⁶). Notice also that 50⁴¹⁻³ is borrowed from 6²²⁻⁴, and 51¹⁵⁻¹⁹ from 10¹²⁻¹⁶.

50². '*standard*'. Cf. 4⁶ and comment there.

'*Bel*'. This is Marduk ('*Merodach*'), the chief god of the Chaldeans, the great sun-god. Cf. 51⁴⁴. See *Bel and the Dragon* in the Apocrypha.

50³. '*out of the north*'. Babylon had come upon Judah from the north, but the time is coming when Babylon's own enemy will arise out of the mysterious '*north*' (cf. verses 9, 41, 4⁶⁻⁷, Isa 46¹⁻²). See commentary above on 1¹³.

50⁷. '*the habitation of justice*'. Better 'their true habitation' (*RSV*). Cf. 2³.

50⁸. '*he-goats*'. These were the leaders of the flocks.

50⁹. '*none shall return*'. Better, 'who does not return'; cf. *RV*m. Follow *RV*m also in 50¹¹, ¹⁵, ²⁶.

50¹⁸. '*As I have punished . . .*'. Nineveh had fallen in 612 B C.

50²¹. The poet is making puns on the names of parts of Babylonia. See *RV*m.

50²⁸. The destruction of Babylon is here taken to be His '*vengeance*' for the destruction of the temple! This is one of a number of indications that this anthology of oracles on Babylon was compiled by those who did not fully understand the message of Jeremiah (cf. Mt. 23²⁹⁻³⁰).

50³⁰. Cf. 49²⁶.

50³¹⁻². Cf. 21¹³⁻¹⁴.

50³⁴. '*redeemer*'. The Lord is their *go'el*: see 32⁷ and commentary there.

50³⁶. '*boasters*'. Read, 'A sword is upon the soothsayers, and they shall become fools'.

50³⁸. '*they are mad upon idols*'. The *ziggurat* of Marduk (the 'tower of Babel') soared like a mountain above the city of Babylon and the flat plain of the Euphrates. It was built by Nabopolassar and his son Nebuchadrezzar. Its terraced mass rose to a height of 288 feet. In the temple, on the lower terrace, was a likeness of Marduk, half animal and half human, made of gold, seated on a throne and with a footstool, beside a table, and all these also made of gold. The 'Gate of Ishtar' was covered with over 500 gay enamelled reliefs of sacred animals, bulls and 'dragons'. All this must have made a great impression on the exiles from Judah. For those who eventually went back to Jerusalem, Babylon became a legend of human pride which snatches at equality with God (see Gen 11 ²⁻⁴, ⁹).

50³⁹. '*wolves*'. Probably 'jackals' (see *RV*m; cf. Isa 13¹⁹⁻²², 34¹¹⁻¹⁷).

50⁴⁴. Cf. 49¹⁹⁻²¹.

51¹. 'Leb-kamai'. A cypher for Chaldea (see *RV*m and cf. verse 41).

51². '*fan*'. Better, 'winnow'; cf. 4¹¹, 15¹.

51⁵. '*their land*'. The land of the Chaldeans.

51⁷. Cf. 25¹⁵⁻¹⁷.

51¹¹. '*hold firm*'. Better, 'prepare'.
'*shields*'. This is better than 'suits of armour' (*RV*m). They were small, circular bucklers.
'*Medes*'. There was a strong expectation that the Medes would attack Babylon in 560 BC, but this did not happen. Cf. verse 28. The author of *Daniel* makes the mistake of assuming that this prophecy was fulfilled.

51¹³. '*the measure of thy covetousness*'. Better, 'the thread of thy life is cut'; cf. *RSV*.

M

51¹⁴. '*cankerworm*'. This is the 'locust. See verse 27.

51²⁰. '*battle axe*'. This is a 'hammer' (cf. *RV*m). See **50²³**. This verse may be addressed to Cyrus (cf. Isa 41 ²⁻⁴).

51²⁶. Cf. **25¹².**

51²⁷. '*standard*'. See commentary on **4⁶**.
'*Ararat, Minni, and Ashkenaz*'. Peoples in the north of the Chaldean empire.
'*marshal*'. A recruiting officer.

51³¹. '*post*'. A royal messenger.

51³². Read 'The fords are captured and the bulwarks have been burned'. Cf. *RV*m and *RSV*.

51³⁴. '*swallowed me up*', '*cast me out*'. Here we have the metaphor which is worked out in the tale of Jonah and the great fish. See Jonah 1 ¹⁷-2 ¹⁰ (cf. verse 44, 9¹¹, 10²², 18¹⁶, Isa 51 ⁹⁻¹¹, 27¹).

51³⁷. '*heaps*'. 'Close by the hill of *Babil* . . . a wooden board at the side of the line announces simply: "Babylon Halt. Trains stop here to pick up passengers". The traveller has arrived at Babylon, and his first impression of what was once the greatest capital of the ancient world is that placard. Not even a station—merely a "halt"!' (A. Parrot, *Discovering Buried Worlds*, p. 118).

51⁴¹. Cf. **25²⁶**, 6²²⁻⁴.

51⁴³. Cf. 2⁶.

51⁴⁴. '*the wall of Babylon*'. This did not in fact fall to Cyrus, though it was destroyed later. It formed the most massive fortification of the ancient world and constituted Babylon the largest walled city that the world has ever seen.

51⁴⁹. Read 'Just as the slain of all the earth have fallen for Babylon, so Babylon is to fall for the slain of Israel'. See *RV*m.

51⁵⁸. '*and they shall be weary*'. See verse 64. At one stage in the editing, this verse was the end of the collection of oracles ascribed to Jeremiah. See commentary on **25¹⁵⁻³⁸**.

51⁵⁹⁻⁶⁴: Jeremiah's sign concerning the end of Babylon

In the fourth year of Zedekiah's reign, the prophet writes his oracles concerning the end of Babylon on a scroll. He gives this to Seraiah, who is going with a delegation from Judah to Babylon. Seraiah is to tie the scroll to a stone and throw it into the Euphrates, as a sign that the time shall come when Babylon sinks, never to rise again.

51⁵⁹. '*the son of Neriah*'. Probably the brother of Baruch; cf. commentary on **45¹⁻⁵**, and **32¹²**.
  '*chief chamberlain*'. Better, 'quartermaster' (*RV*m).

51⁶⁰. '*in a book*'. On a scroll. What the prophet writes is what the Lord has '*spoken*' (verse 61). See commentary on **36¹⁻³²**.

51⁶¹. '*read*'. Read *aloud*.

51⁶⁴. '*Thus far are the words of Jeremiah*'. An editorial indication that chapter **52** is an historical appendix and not an account of the acts or the sayings of the prophet. The phrase was probably transferred at some stage from verse **58**, and this accounts for the repetition here of the phrase '*and they shall be weary*'.

The intention of this sign may have been to discourage the court of Zedekiah from further intrigue against Babylon by assuring them that, if they will only be patient and trust the Lord, the time will certainly come when He will bring the domination of Babylon to an end. This is another of Jeremiah's 'visual aids', a dramatic prophecy, an action which was believed to be the real beginning of the fulfilment of what was predicted.

What is the preacher to make of this collection of sayings about Babylon in chapters **50-1**? Before we become too self-righteous about the indications that some of the compilers of these sayings seem to have cherished a desire for vengeance, we have to recall with shame some of the things that were

said and done by some Christians in times of war in this
twentieth century. We know better than people did in the
day of Nebuchadrezzar and Cyrus, but we do not always do
better. We may have to oppose our enemies and struggle against
them, but we are never free to cease to love them, or to cease
to desire their peace in a true reconciliation, according to the
will of God. We must not fall into the habit of regarding the
USSR or China as 'Babylon' to be destroyed in a holy war.
We must recognize, as Jeremiah would have done, that they
may be God's instruments for correcting much of our way
of life, even though they must eventually fall if they persist
in boasting against their true Lord (cf. Isa 10[5-7]). Even if our
Nebuchadrezzars seem to have something of the might of the
monster of chaos (the '*dragon*' of 51[34]), we know that the Lord
is '*the former of all things*' (51[19]), the Victor over chaos who
shapes the whole universe according to His own design (cf.
10[16], Ps 103[19]). He has the whole world, and all the worlds,
'in His hand'. Therefore we owe it to Babylon to make it
clear that it is dangerous for her to behave as if she is God and
so to strive '*against the Lord*' (50[24]). Only when we are loving
our enemies, and paying them the debt we owe to them of
declaring in word and deed that there is a righteous God who
is the Only Judge and Saviour, have we the right to rejoice
that '*Israel is not forsaken, nor Judah, of his God, of the Lord of
hosts*' (51[5]). We owe it to every form of power in the modern
world that is working against God, and against His people
—commercialized superstition, traffic in drink and in drugs,
gambling industries and many others, known and unknown—
to make it plain that we believe in a Lord who 'appeared for
the very purpose of undoing the devil's work' (1 Jn 3[8], *NEB*).
Every Babylon that sets itself up against Him has posted up
its own death sentence: the time is coming when they shall
'*sink*' and '*not rise again*' (51[64]), and the Lord will '*give rest
to the earth*' (50[34]). The monsters are on the beaten side and
our faith is that nothing in the created universe is 'able to
separate us from the love of God, which is in Christ Jesus
our Lord' (cf. Rom 8[37-9]). It is not for us to know when or
how it may happen that the evil will be destroyed. (51[11, 29]
were not fulfilled as their author expected, since Cyrus conquered the Medes as well as the Babylonians, and he and his
victorious Persians did not sack the city of Babylon in 538
BC.) But we can fulfil part of our debt of love to our enemies

by living in the faith that 'Jesus the Judge shall come' and that
even now,

> *He sits at God's right hand,*
> *Till all His foes submit.* (*MHB* 247)

God's people are still those who have accepted His offer of an
'*everlasting covenant*' and they '*inquire concerning Zion with
their faces thitherward*' (**50⁵**). Since their life is founded on the
fact that He has blotted out their sin and cast it behind His
back (**50²⁰**, cf. **31³⁴**), they know that there is no room for the
man who asks the way to true life with his face still turned to
the world. It is pointless to be Mr. Facing-both-ways, to try
to serve God and Mammon. For it is the Lord who is the 'true
habitation' of His people (*RSV* of **50⁷**); our hearts are restless
until they find their rest in Him. True life means that we dwell
in Him for evermore, and He in us. The gospel is that the Lord
is the *go'el*, the '*redeemer*' (**50³⁴**) who has related Himself
to us in such a way that we can depend on Him for deliverance
and protection. He is the Kinsman who has shown His readiness 'to pay the price of sin' and accept us as 'joint-heirs' with
Himself. He it is who stands for us over against all the might
of 'Babylon', and His kingdom is an everlasting kingdom (cf.
Ps 72¹²⁻¹⁴, *RV*m of Job 19²⁵).

'*Thus far are the words of Jeremiah*' (verse 64). When God
speaks to His prophets, it is in relation to things as they are.
So, when the things that were said to a prophet twenty-five
centuries ago come to us as the word of God, they come, not
simply as bits of historical or biographical or psychological
knowledge, but in relation to things as they are now. Jeremiah
shows us the terrible possibilities that can arise from not seeking
first the Kingdom of God. We see him now as a noble brave
'*iron pillar*' (**1¹⁸**), a man whose life was 'founded upon the
rock' (Mt 7²⁵). But today also, anyone who is loyal to his
Lord may be faced with a call to similar bravery. We may
have to stand for the whole Christian fellowship to which we
belong over against some folly of nationalism, or even against
some corruption of the Church.

There is something fundamentally wrong with our society,
as there was with Judah. What seemed once to be 'benefits
of civilization'—science and medicine, education and prosperity, new sources of power and increased leisure—can be
used for good or for evil. We do not know whether God's

way for the world tomorrow will have to be peace or trouble. But, whatever happens, we must repent. We do know that this is one of the things for which we must stand in the power of the Holy Spirit—repentance, a change of '*heart*', conversion into the way of righteousness and mercy. This is possible, because the Lord stands, righteous and merciful, above all the perplexity and confusion of our times. He is the Mighty Comforter whose love never comes to an end, the Faithful One to whom we can trust everything, the one Lord to whom the final word belongs, even Jesus Christ our Saviour.

IV. Historical appendix

52¹⁻³⁴: The end of the kingdom of Judah

How Jerusalem fell and Zedekiah was taken into exile. How Evil-merodach became emperor of Babylonia and released ex-king Jehoiachin from prison and gave him good treatment for the rest of his days.

52¹². '*the fifth month*'. Probably of a year reckoned from the spring, i.e. August.

52¹⁵. '*multitude*'. Better, 'artificers' (*RV*m). It is the rest of the craftsmen who are taken away.

52²⁰. '*under the bases*'. This should probably be 'under the sea' (cf. *RSV*); see verse 17.
   '*without weight*'. Better, 'not weighed' or with *RSV* 'beyond weight'.

52²¹. '*a line of twelve cubits did compass it*'. It was about eighteen feet in circumference.
   '*fingers*'. This is the only place in the Bible where this small unit (one twenty-fourth of a cubit) is mentioned.

52²². '*chapiter*'. The 'capital' at the top of the pillar.

52²⁴. These are all the chief officials of the Temple.

52³¹. *'lifted up the head'*. He gave honourable treatment to Jehoiachin (cf. Gen 40¹³, ²⁰).

52³³. *'before him'*. As a member of the Chaldean king's court.

This historical appendix is heavily dependent on 2 Kings 24¹⁸-25³⁰, though there are some differences (cf. *RV*m of verses 1, 31. See also 2 Chr 35²⁰-36²¹). The most important difference is the information about the numbers of people carried off to Babylon, given in verses 28-30. Three deportations are mentioned, the third of them coming after Johanan and his group had taken the prophet and Baruch into Egypt (verse 30). The total of *'four thousand and six hundred'* seems more likely to be near the truth than the figure of about 20,000 which is suggested in 2 Kings. A commentary on 2 Kings should be consulted. Verses 28-30 are not included in the *LXX*.

So the book ends with this historical account of how the prophecies of Jeremiah relating to the destruction of Jerusalem were fulfilled. Concerning the fulfilment of his prophecies of hope, the historian of Judah has nothing to report. . . .

We are at the end of a journey through this book of prophecy which to some readers may seem to have the faults of a fast trip by car—there has been little time to take in the beauty and significance of the country through which we have passed. But even if this journey is ended, the road is still there, and the reader is free to go back over it, and travel as slowly as he desires. It will always be worthwhile—though never comfortable—to travel through the Book of *Jeremiah*. Each time we do so, we come to know the prophet better, and to admire, and marvel at him. We come to sympathize with, and to love, this man who lived over 2,500 years ago, because he served his God and ours. The record of his sufferings, sorrows and consolations in that service is his monument. It is a monument that points us, not to Jeremiah, but to the One who made him, to the Lord who is eternally praised by all the goodly fellowship of the prophets, in the fellowship of His *'council'*.

Index

Index

Abiathar, 1, 7, 24
Advent, 13, 58, 71
Affluent society, 160
Almond branch, 11f
Amen, 33
Amos, 9
Anath, 43, 152
Anathoth, 1, 7, 62f, 128, 130
Apostolic Succession, 103
Ark, 24, 43
Asherah, 19, 43, 80
Assyria, 1, 17, 106
Atheism, 35
Authority, 99, 112

Baal, 15, 24, 25, 36, 53, 129
Babylon, 59, 165ff
Babylonia, 91, 113f, 151, 155, 163ff
Baruch, 111, 129, 137, 138, 149,
    153f, 167
Bible Sunday, 138
Bonhoeffer, D., 78, 141, 144
Bride of the Lord, 15f, 24, 61, 69,
    78, 123, 126

Calling. See Election
Carchemish, 2, 5, 91, 106, 138, 155
chesed. See Love of God
Circumcision, 27f, 56f
Civilization, 169f
Community, 36, 77, 104, 122ff,
    127. See Fellowship
Congo, 146
Conversion, 25f, 27, 120, 123, 125,
    170
Covenant, 43, 46, 60f, 63, 84, 91,
    108, 121, 122f, 123ff, 134, 155
Covetousness, 39
Creator, 13, 36f, 50f, 58, 60, 66,
    87f, 128, 145, 152, 163, 168. See
    Nature.

Discipline, 79, 119f

Election, 9f, 16, 63, 66, 75f, 82, 85f,
    124f
Enemies, 63, 75, 83, 110, 113, 167f
Exodus, 16, 99, 128, 155

Faith, 46, 75f, 81f, 93f, 115, 120,
    126, 131, 153
Faithfulness. See Love of God
Fear, 116
Fellowship, 59, 77, 102f, 108, 124.
    See Community
Flesh, 81
Forgiveness, 125, 127
Freedom, 112

Gedaliah, 2, 5, 117, 145ff
Gehenna, 44, 122f
Gentiles, 58, 105, 111f, 113, 147
George the Fifth, 31

Harvest, 51f
Heart, 27f, 32, 35, 37, 56, 64, 65,
    80ff, 104, 122, 125f, 128
Hell. See Gehenna
Holy, 16
Hosea, 15
Hoyle, Fred, 60

Idolatry, 20f, 39, 57ff, 79, 105, 160
Individual, 76, 77, 103, 123f
Intercession, 45, 48f, 71, 73, 74,
    88, 95, 113
Ishtar, 43, 152
Israel, 17, 28f, 115ff, 121f

Jews, 66
Jonah, 150
Judgement, 39, 54f, 100, 107f, 169
Justice, 10, 55, 100

Kenya, 146
Knowledge, 14, 28, 30, 52, 54f, 62,
    79, 100, 102, 114, 122, 125f

Lamentations, 2
Leisure, 84
Loneliness, 78
Lord's Day, 84
Love of God, 14ff, 24, 26, 54, 74, 75, 116, 117f, 136, 153, 170
Luther, Martin, 45, 110, 139, 141

Marcion, 139
Mercy. *See* Love of God
Messiah, 97-100
Mission of the Church, 14, 66, 68f, 78f, 86, 100, 105, 108, 118, 126, 128, 142, 146, 147
Morality, 55

Nature, 36f, 87f, 111, 117. *See* Creator
New Covenant. *See* Covenant
New Year, 51f
Nuclear weapons, 31, 91, 100

On the Beach, 25

Patience, 153
Peace, 10, 39f, 50f, 63, 72, 77, 79, 114, 133, 145
Perfection, 77, 124
Pessimism, 70
Politics, 10, 14, 60
Predestination. *See* Election
Pride, 68, 159ff, 165
Priest, 88, 92
Promises, 135

Prophecy, prophet (true and false), 13, 72, 73, 88, 92, 101ff, 110f, 112ff, 130, 138, 149, 169

Religion, 19f, 26, 45, 46f, 60, 80, 102, 116, 152
Repentance, 20ff, 25f, 27f, 74, 77, 84f, 120, 170
Revelation, 14, 130
Righteousness, 54f, 98, 100, 133

Sabbath, 84
Sacrifice, 11, 35, 45ff, 61, 90f
Salvation, 53, 116, 120, 124f, 169f
Scythians, 12
Security, 44, 46, 59, 65, 96, 105, 112, 150, 160
Shepherd, 17, 58, 69, 97, 98, 119, 120
Sin, 19, 20, 28, 36, 54, 70, 125, 133
Slavery, 134f
Stewardship, 46, 84
Suffering, 31f, 52f, 65, 71, 93, 154

Temple, 3, 42, 45ff, 109f
Tradition, 46f, 136
Trinity Sunday, 104
Truth, 33, 54, 144
Tyndale, 139

Visitation, 58
Vocation. *See* Election

Wisdom, 81f
Worship, 41, 46f, 80f
Wrath, 68, 107f, 119f